A Garden Manifesto

A Garden Manifesto

Edited by Olivia Laing
and Richard Porter

PILOT PRESS

A Garden Manifesto

No, the wild tulip shall outlast the prison wall
no matter what grows within.
John Wieners

On 20 May at 16:35 I texted Richard Porter, the publisher of Pilot Press. I was on a train to Southampton, in the third week of *The Garden Against Time* book tour. "I might have just had an idea," I wrote. "Do you want to do an anthology called *A Garden Manifesto*? And we could co-edit? Focus on radical dreams for the future rooted in the earth." I'd been travelling around the country talking to gardeners, writers, artists, readers, and I was bursting with the sense that something was happening out there. There was clearly a sea-change in how people were gardening, particularly in environmental terms, but there was also a fierce interest in the garden as political metaphor.

What I had in mind was a container for all kinds of different and disparate things: not a party line so much as a seed box of ideas. I looked out of the window of the train and realised I was passing Twyford Down, the birthplace of the road protest movement in the UK. "Let's do it," Rich texted back.

We wanted the book to feel more like a zine than a formal anthology, and we wanted to make it quickly. We met at the end of May in London and assembled a wish list of contributors, some living, some dead, some close to us and some total strangers. Then we started sending out invitations.

A Garden Manifesto is a collection of dreams of the past and visions for the future, both personal and political. We'd welcome photos, manifestos, memories, poems, drawings, lists and planting plans. What have gardens meant to you? How do you envisage gardens changing the world? Please feel free to think of gardens as literal places or metaphors for a better society, gardens as lost or reclaimed Edens, gardens as sites of pleasure, freedom, complexity and abundance. We want to capture the radical ideas of the summer of 2024 and store them as a seed box for an uncertain future.

The first reply came in 37 minutes. Almost everyone we asked said yes. The garden is a place of generosity and it felt like people responded with the same spirit of abundance and immediacy. In the early 1990s I was involved with the riot grrrl fanzine scene, and I'm not sure any project I've been a part of until now has matched that spirit of open-handed, super-energetic collaboration.

If I were to trace out some of the themes and preoccupations of these pages, I might think first of home-making, of the way plants can help people to feel rooted when they are estranged or severed from their home. From Gaylene Gould's breadfruit to Kuba Ryniewicz's paper apples to the remarkable Palestinian Heirloom Seed Library, plants are potent ways of reckoning with experiences of exile and loss, of resisting colonial violence and salvaging the essence of a loved origin place. To borrow a phrase from the great poet of the enclosures, John Clare, "the axe of the spoiler and self-interest" has destroyed far too much of our planet. But as Clare also knew, growing gardens, planting flowers and cherishing the landscape is a potent way of reclaiming Eden from the despoilers.

This latter urge is also at play in the many images and narratives we gathered of DIY Eden-making, be it gardens built on vacant lots in New York City, alternative communities established in third-growth redwood forests or seeds scattered in Long Kesh, Belfast, on the site of the notoriously brutal former prison HMP Maze. Please feast on these records of resistance and glorious refusal, perhaps best exemplified by Gerry Dalton, the Irish immigrant who built an idiosyncratic garden of hand-cast concrete statues on what had been a rubbish dump behind his council flat in West London. The world can always be made more beautiful, more strange, more open, and each one of us can participate, simply by being willing to sow seed, to articulate our dreams.

Time is also a recurrent preoccupation. The garden can be a time-capsule, a way of re-encountering the past (think of Philip Hoare's spinster day-trippers, Misses Moberley and Jourdain, coming face to face with a long-dead queen in the grounds of Versailles). Gardens outlive their owners, converting us to ghosts, and provide a way of reckoning with mortality, exceeding the smallness of our human lives. As Eileen Myles puts it, "What I think is going on is that I am growing something that will keep growing when *I* die." At the same time, they are also laboratories, sites for generating new ideas and processes that can shape the future, often in unexpected ways. Lots of ideas here for what that future might be.

Pilot Press is an explicitly queer publishing house and Rich and I noticed as we were assembling the layout on my studio floor that much of this book could be read as a kind of queer family tree, connected by lines of affinity rather than ties of blood. Some of the contributors are or were actual friends, while others speak to each other across the centuries, through a tissue of shared preoccupations that are to do with both pleasure and loss, eroticism, hope and rage. I'm sure you as reader will find your own chain of connections and correspondences as you leaf through.

People have been asking me a lot lately how I think we can achieve Eden now, in a century that is already being violently reshaped by climate change. Reverse the enclosures, obviously. Undo the severance from nature that was and is such a key part of the colonial project, as essays by Sui Searle, Hussein Omar, Claire Ratinon and Gaylene Gould make clear. Create public gardens in all our cities, to act as biodiverse habitat and climate-resilient protection against heatwaves and floods, as well as sites of conviviality and peacefulness.

But what this anthology really conveys is the importance, the true vitality, of the idiosyncratic response: the passionate, the intimate, the local. I don't mean individualism, because many of the projects documented here are collective. I mean that they come from the ground up. The gardens we've assembled are not homogenised, and definitely not for profit. They're anarchic and defiant, free for all. They include you.

Olivia Laing, August 2024

Poem to be written on a tombstone

Wah! How-every time the plants in the garden
Sprouted-glad became my heart.
Pass by, O friend, that in the spring
Thou mayest see plants sprouting from my loam.

Saadi
From *The Golestan of Saadi,* 1258 CE
Translated by Richard Francis Burton

Joe Brainard
Madonna with Flowers IV, 1966
Gouache and collage on paper

Courtesy of the Estate of Joe Brainard

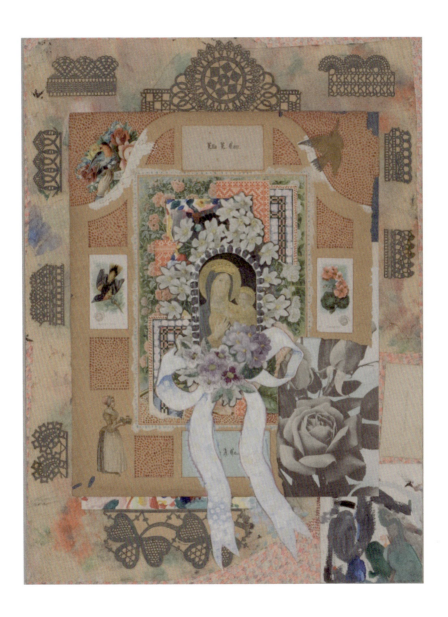

Ella E. Carr.

11

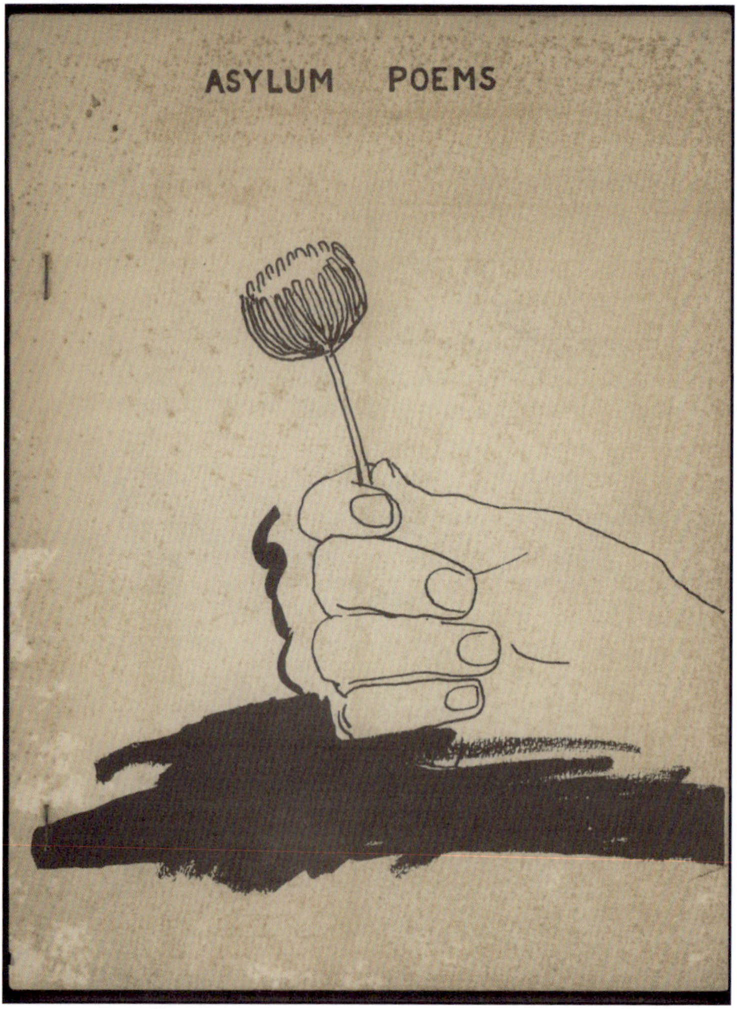
ASYLUM POEMS

Private Estate

Dancing dandelions
and buttercups in the grass
remind me of other summer
flowers, simple blossoms

roses and tiger lilies by the wall
　　　milk pod, sumac branches
lilacs across the road, daisies, blueberries
snaps, cut violets

　　　three years ago still grow in my mind
as peonies or planted geraniums, bachelor buttons
in downy fields filled with clover
lover, come again and again up fern

path upheld as memory's perennial
against stern hard-faced officers of imprisonment
and cold regulation more painful than lover's arms
or flowers charming but not more lasting.

No, the wild tulip shall outlast the prison wall
no matter what grows within.

6.21.69

John Wieners
From *Asylum Poems*, Angel Hair Books, 1969

Violets

Every year a patch of violets appears on the canal on the walk to my studio
– it's early spring – the first sign I always think – although I also think
about someone telling me that they grow lushly in graveyards and I wonder
if there are bodies buried there, so many grow there, and I think of Eliot
even though that's lilacs…that year I stole some and tried to paint them
(hiding them in my pocket conscious of how wrong it is to pick wild
flowers) – they also make me think of Manet's paintings of Berthe Morisot
and Paula Modersohn-Becker's violets in an egg cup and novels with girls
selling bunches of violets for 6 pence and cheap perfume and violet creams,
which you don't see any more and I never liked and more than most flowers
they are about the shortness of life, no sooner have you picked them, their
thin delicate stems and heavy heads begin to droop and die.

Chantal Joffe
Violets, 2019
Oil on board

Courtesy of the artist

14

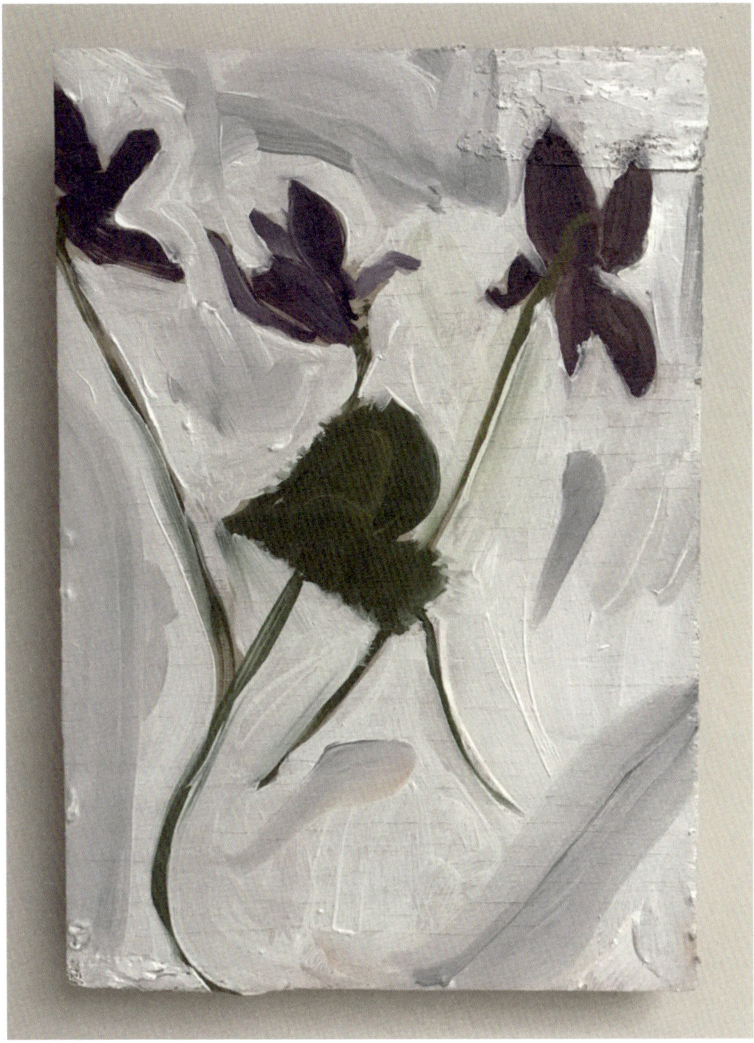

Gardening to remember

As a gardener and creator of the @decolonisethegarden Instagram account and the online substack newsletter, Radicle, one of the things that preoccupies me is: What do I do this for anyway (this gardening thing, that is)? How might I be doing things better or differently? Healthier for me, for my kin (both human and more-than-human), and for the planet?

I find it fascinating to look more fundamentally at how and why we garden. The framing and narratives we tell ourselves. Our intention. And how this might be something useful or interesting to think about in these times of crises and division facing us.

I'm particularly interested in the story of separation that we tell ourselves. Something that, once you see it, you could say is at the root of many of the issues facing us today: from the climate crisis, to biodiversity loss, to our broken food system, to our health crisis, to our gross over-consumption-driven society, to racism and exploitation, even to burn-out and worsening mental health.

My journey into gardening began almost 20 years ago, when I retrained as a career-changer. I was miserable in an office job in the city, wondering how I could possibly bear to spend the rest of my days writing reports and attending seemingly endless strategy meetings. I felt flattened and dulled by the greyness and sterility of corporate, office life; weighed down by all the glass and concrete surrounding me in an urban environment. I had this yearning for something with more meaning. I wanted to feel as though I was making a positive difference. I wanted to be more outdoors, to feel connected to the seasons, landscape, the earth, the natural world: I wanted more connection to "nature".

When I started my gardening career though, there were many things to contend with that I hadn't factored for and feelings of being, I suppose, regularly compromised. As gardeners we didn't always do what was best for "nature". As with everyone and everything else, we were driven by a seeming scarcity of time and money and a belief that "nature" was something there to be dominated and controlled and put to use for our needs.

I had this creeping feeling that the thing I thought I had changed careers to do - to be greener, to be more in touch with nature - was not turning out to be the reality. Everything, in the end, seemed to come down to time and money and manipulating, abusing or extracting from "nature" for our own ends and often for little more than a sense of style, aesthetics, standards, politeness or conformity - and to make a profit.

Mowing lawns (veritable resource/energy intensive & hungry mono-cultures) constantly for the sake of tidiness and appearances. Trimming hedges at times when you wouldn't out of choice - in bird nesting season for example. Putting in metres of irrigation systems for wealthy clients who didn't have time or inclination to care for their garden but wanted a high enough status, lush, outdoor garden room to accompany expensive and immaculate homes. Endless plastic bought and discarded with little thought or care. Pesticides and herbicides used as standard gardening practice. Ripping up the existing or the old just to lay down something new and shiny with little thought for waste, emissions, resources, repurposing or salvaging. I wasn't really sure how any of this was working with or for the benefit of "nature" and of course, it often wasn't.

Things have started changing, slowly. There is a greater awareness, mostly of environmental concerns. We are more willing to let lawns and verges grow. People are beginning to see "weeds" for the invaluable plants that they are… But it wasn't until only relatively recently that I began to really understand a truth that I think I had long been feeling in my body. That our very view, our way of seeing and being in the world, is out of alignment and making us behave in questionable ways. It is what was fuelling this sense of disconnection that so many of us feel.

Something really shifted for me in particular after listening to a talk given by Rebecca Hosking (a regenerative farmer based in Devon), which she gave for the Oxford Real Farming Conference (ORFC) a few years ago. She talked about how language frames our way of thinking and affects our behaviour. Words such as "nature", "weeds" and "pests" is the language of mastery and dominance. It reflects our broken, destructive, abusive relationship with the rest of life on Earth.

Our behaviour is influenced by our thought processes, which is shaped by the words and stories and metaphors we use. She said how in many indigenous cultures there is no separation between humans and "nature". In fact many do not even have an equivalent word.

Things began to fall into place in my mind.

As humans, we like to make meaning, create myths and tell stories. They affect how we see ourselves, our place in the world and also how we behave: more essentially, how we choose to live in relation to each other, the land, even our food and governance systems. Alnoor Ladha talks about how our collective imaginary has been completely shaped and limited by neo-capitalism, how every aspect of our lives is mediated by money. He talks about the importance of being good students of our culture and understanding the context within which we are enmeshed and that this starts by understanding our ontology or our theory of being. That is, the way we understand reality.

This makes complete sense to me. To try to understand the root of something.

Why do we behave the way we do? What stories are we telling ourselves?

One of the fundamental stories we tell ourselves, or myths that we believe, is one of separation and division.

This idea that there is this thing called "nature", that we are separate from, is our dominant way of seeing the world. We humans (in the west) see ourselves as separate from and superior to "nature".

Since the birth of Western science, during the Enlightenment, this biased, colonial idea of "modern", with a greater separation from "nature" being seen as a sign of superiority, human progress and "development" has been pervasive and to this day it affects, is even used to justify, how we judge and oppress other cultures and people.

This language of separation is our dominant language. Just as we are also dominated by a rationalist view - a belief that the world can be reduced into comprehension by the human mind.

I'm interested in how, with greater awareness, might gardening help to heal some of our wounds, narratives and disconnection. Perhaps it can point us towards different ways of seeing and being in this world. In other words, to decolonise.

Ladha talks about understanding the ontology within which we are enmeshed and practising a liberation ontology. Like so much that gardening can provide us with space to hold and process, I believe that it is a site in which we can begin to practice a liberation ontology.

If our existing ontology - or way of seeing the world - seeks to divide and separate us, could gardening help to reconnect us? Robin Wall-Kimmerer at least thinks so. As she says in her book, Braiding Sweetgrass:

People often ask me what one thing I would recommend to restore relationship between land and people. My answer is almost always, "Plant a garden." It's good for the health of the earth and it's good for the health of people. A garden is a nursery for nurturing connection, the soil for cultivation of practical reverence. And its power goes far beyond the garden gate—once you develop a relationship with a little patch of earth, it becomes a seed itself.

Put in more practical terms, a liberatory way would be to practise power WITH, rather than power OVER. This is what is called liberatory power (as opposed to oppressive power). How do we build regenerative systems in "power with" our kin - our fellow living beings - rather than reinforcing destructive, extractive ones in our gardening practice and beyond?

I believe that gardening - consciously, intentionally - could help us to see differently. When we see kin, we see, think, feel, behave differently. But this doesn't just happen. It isn't a passive thing. It requires practice, which has to be continuous. It requires a consciousness. Kin, or to make it a verb - kinning - requires doing since becoming kin is relational.

How do I choose to see, and be in relation with, the plants and wildlife around me in my garden?

When I garden I do so trying to nurture a connectedness and kinship to the more-than-human, to the earth I plant into, to the place I am situated in and all the beings around me. And I don't think that this action and intention is insignificant.

As Judy Ling Wong says: "we love what we enjoy and we want to protect what we love". Gardening, through this enjoyment, cultivates love. It can help us to find ways back to connection with this earth, ourselves and each other. When you love something, you care for it - and so it is with gardening and tending the earth and habitat we share with other beings. In our garden ecosystems we can see how our flourishing is closely intertwined and connected with the rest of life.

Practising a liberatory ontology and cultivating kinship has to encompass all our ways of thinking, being and doing. It includes how we see and treat all our fellow humans and all our more-than-human kin in the rest of the living world. It is not instant, it is not easy. For sure, it is an ongoing practice, made harder by the fact that we don't have a culture that recognises kinship with plants, seeing them instead as passive and insentient.

Gavin Van Horn points out that caring for small wonders is within reach of us all and that the world needs caretakers, not saviours. He asks us: "what is within reach?" And I think gardening can help us do that - it focuses us on what is within reach. What can we do, how can we care, in our own backyards and green patches - and then how might this ripple out beyond?

As Merlin Sheldrake has written, "It is by imagining ourselves as separable - from one another and the ecosystems that sustain us - that we justify both the exploitation and the oppression of other humans and ecological devastation".

When we garden we become more directly connected to the web of life, strengthening our relationship to ourselves and with all living beings, human or otherwise, around us.

I believe that gardening with intention can help us to remember our connection - perhaps even, to remember ourselves as a limb of a larger body or whole. We are not separate or superior. We are all indigenous to Earth. We belong to one another. We all belong here.

Sui Searle

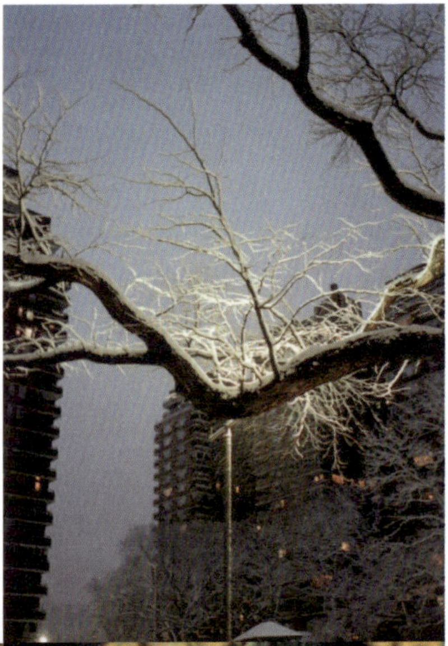

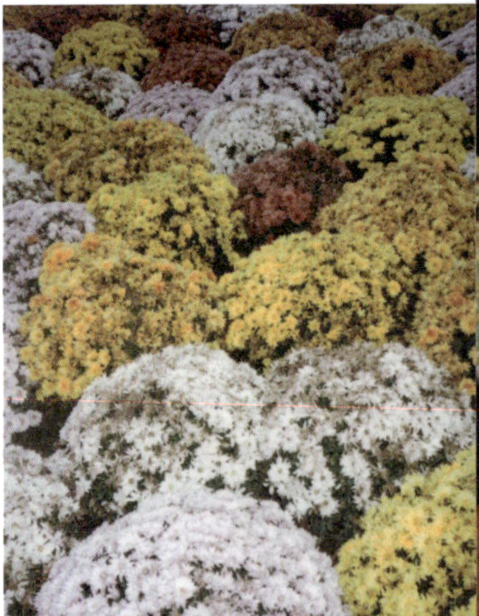

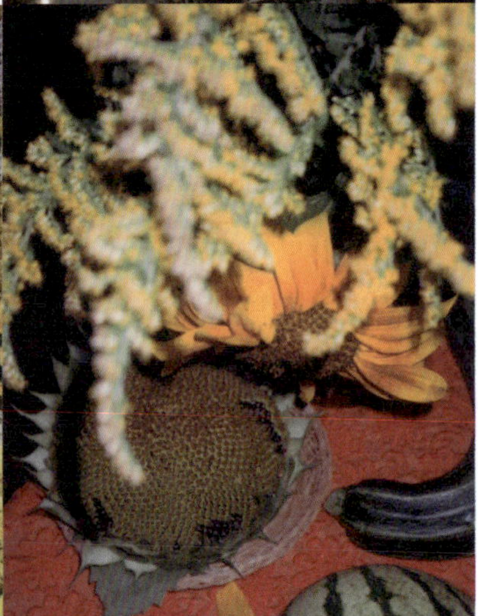

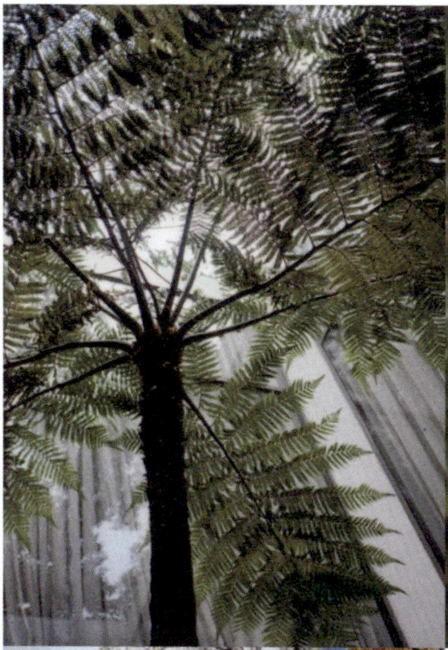
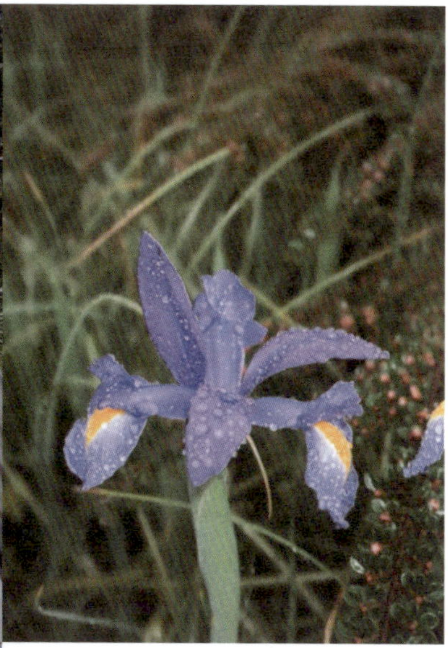
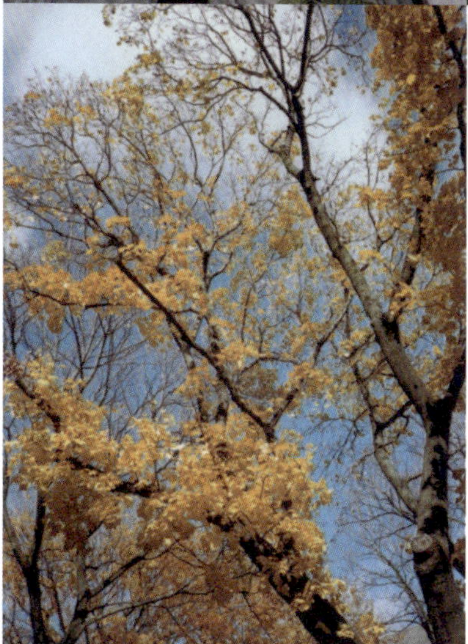

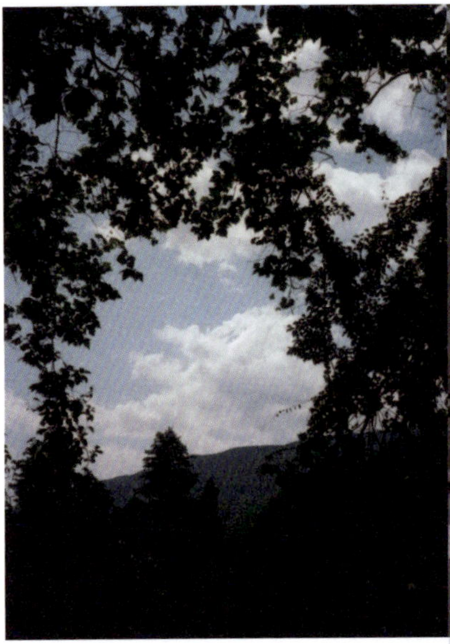

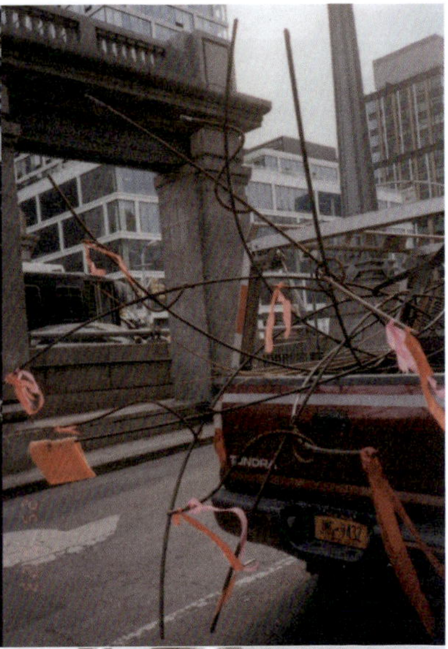

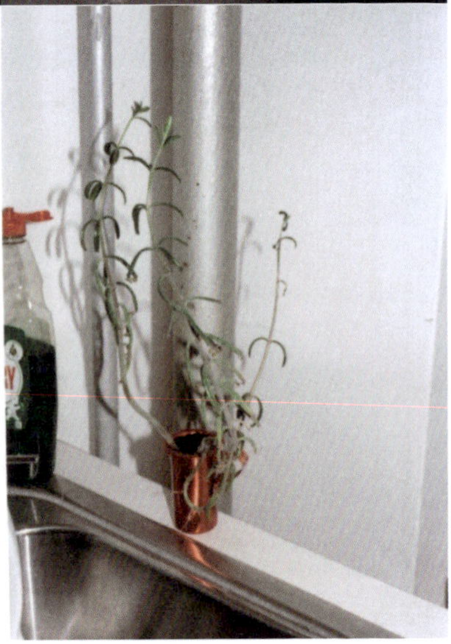

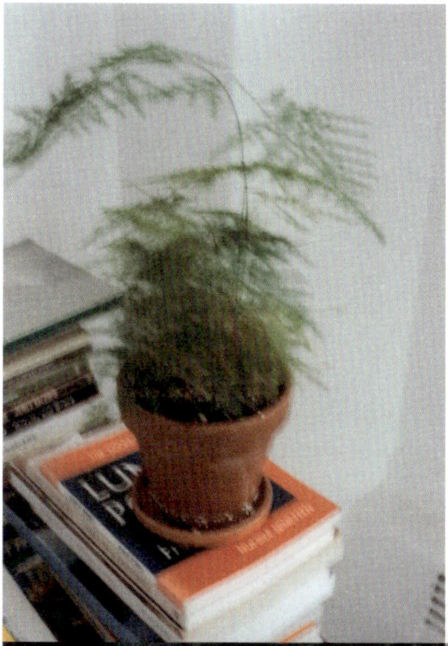

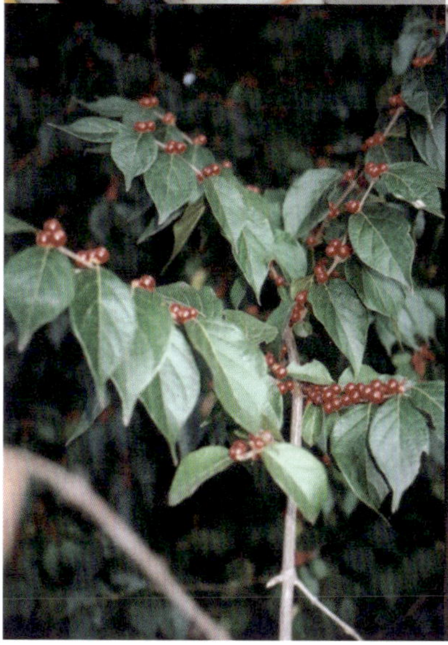

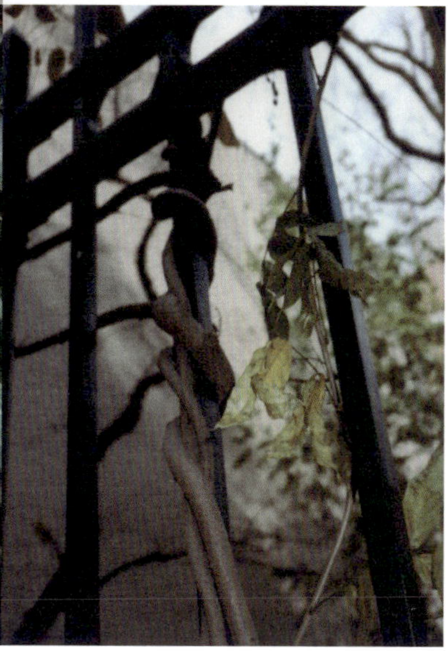

Lee Mary Manning
Untitled series of 35mm film photographs

Courtesy of the artist

Edward Thomasson
The sweet smell of spring dirt, 2023
Pencil, watercolour, coloured pencil, pastel and acrylic on paper

Courtesy of the artist and Phillida Reid, London

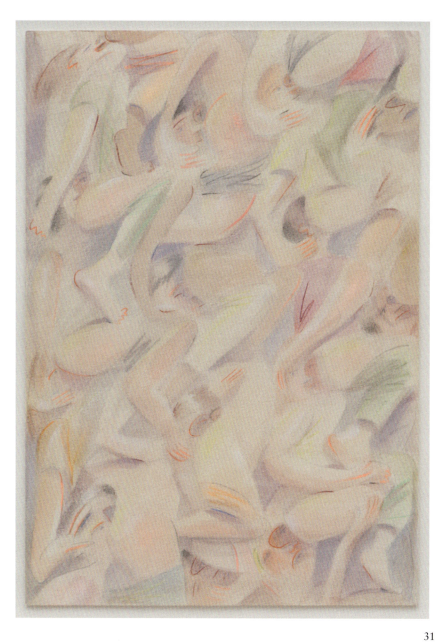

Fertile Soil

Ever since I was a boy, I have felt haunted. I felt I could see and hear ghosts, especially my own. Perhaps it was because I was the last of four brothers and most of the male genes had run out by the time it came to me. Or maybe I was the ghost of the other child I was meant to be. My mother told me, much later in life, that I had been a happy child until a certain point, and then I changed.

Our three-bedroom, semi-detached house in the suburbs was certainly haunted. By the painting of the blue boy at the top of the stairs, a place where neither I nor my younger sisters lingered; and by my second eldest brother, who had died suddenly, at the age of twenty-three. For some strange reason I thought I saw him in the garden, standing under a willow tree. As if he'd grown into it, or it had grown out of him. His cocky head, his Irish bogbrush hair. Flickering, the way that sunlight falls through leaves at midday.

Gardens, being uncontrollable places of shadows and lust, are inevitably haunted, by their former owners, as Olivia Laing vividly and personally attests in her Garden Against Time. But perhaps they are also over-shadowed by their future fates, too, what will happen to them when everyone's gone.

The garden of the house where I was born was haunted by something quite real, since my brothers had dug a giant hole in it and buried an unwanted upright piano in there, rather like the disposal of Arthur Conan Doyle, who insisted on being interred upright like a sunken Easter Island statue. Long after we'd moved to our new house—in which I still live, sixty years on—the people who lived in the old one claimed to hear eerie music as they walked on their lawn.

The garden that I most remember from childhood, where I felt least secure, was my grandmother's garden that stretched round her colonial bungalow in the New Forest. On desultory Sunday afternoons, as we came to make our dutiful visit, while she talked to my mother, her daughter, whom she never really liked, we were allowed to escape Nanny's brown lisle stockings wrinkling around her broomstick-thin legs and run free in her garden.

There the drive and paths were neatly gravelled, giving them the air of the desultory beach that lay a mile or so down the road. Just by the back door was a galvanised water tank, always filled to the brim with stilled rain. I could stand on tiptoe and peer in the dark green water, which might have been without end, bottomless, so far as I was concerned.

My mother's greatest companion as a girl had been her terrier, Peter, so loyal and forbearing that he would allow her to ride on his back. But then came the day when he had grown too old, and fatally ailing, was 'put down' by my grandfather. I never knew how or why this was done (I think I remember a gas poker being involved); but I had the faint if improbable idea that he had been drowned in that tank. I imagined him down there, his paws faintly waving and beckoning from below.

Gardens were fatal because they allowed wilder creatures in. They were the backdoor into my anxieties, essentially uncontrollable, and therefore places of deep and exquisite desire and pain. I remember a slow worm slithering across our lawn. I was gardening with my father, one of the few things we did together. For some reason—perhaps to demonstrate my fugitive masculinity, or my solidarity with St Patrick who so wantonly drove the snakes out of Ireland; or maybe I mistook it for Satan himself, whispering in my ear—I raised the spade with which I was digging and sliced the legless lizard in half.

I regret that anti-Eden act deeply even now, as much as I mourn drowning a hedgehog in a bucket, under the what I now suspect spurious reasoning that the bulging white blob on its eye condemned it to an otherwise lingering death. I held the spiky ball down as the animal drowned, very quickly. Then I chucked it under the privet hedge. Privet hedges, by definition, hide so many private things. Peering neighbours, sex offenders, adders and foxes and many other lost things.

Anything could come into my grandmother's garden, I believe, since there was a secret green room at the back, edged round with a privet hedge that seemed as tall as a castle's walls. I felt I could walk into the green embankments and they'd grow around me whole: the ultimate hiding place in a game of hide and seek. There was a shallow stone bird bath in the middle of this courtyard, where birds never bathed. The cursed semi-suburban beauty of this place seemed bewitched by its efforts to regulate nature. The gated arch cut into the far hedge led directly out into that wilderness where I'd be as irrevocably lost as if I'd drowned at sea.

I connected all these things, fearfully in my head, on those Sunday afternoons; not least because in her glass cabinet, which was otherwise filled with a hundred china dogs, my grandmother kept a hag stone she had found on the beach and which, I was told, was a charm to keep witches at bay. Later we learned that Nanny's husband (it was her second marriage; my real grandfather, who had served in India, and had only one eye, had died long before I was born); that this caddish interloper abused her, on one occasion pouring the contents of a chamber pot over her head.

I was a strange child—who wasn't?—and I have always sensed the unease of an unattended garden; a place made for people without people in it is by default and definition uncanny. Gardens were places which were, in the Edwardian argot of collegiate ghost story tellers, queer. They invite and permit transformation, since they constantly change shape, even as you look at them, never the same from one day to the day. In Nanny's dark garden, I imagined a white hart from the forest leaping over that hedge like a unicorn.

In a book I'd got out of the local library, where our father would take us on early Thursday evenings when it opened until 7 pm to allow working families to access its rows of random volumes covered in prophylactic plastic against communicable diseases, I read about two ladies, Misses Moberly and Jourdain—they would have been called spinsters then, and their close friendship entirely unsuspicious—had gone on a trip to Paris and went to visit Versailles.

It was 1901. The summer was warm and sultry, and the great palace bored Moberly and Jourdain. So they left it to its banal hall of mirrors, which only show you yourself, and using their Baedeker as a guide, tried to find the Petit

Trianon, the replica farm where Marie Antoinette could play at being a real person.

As they walked down a tree-shadowed path, the atmosphere become somehow oppressive—not that they admitted it to each other until long afterwards, when they came to discuss the experience they shared that afternoon. Almost at the edge of their vision, figures seemed to move through the trees—around them. They heard people passing them; they sensed their presence, but did not see anyone. Then they came upon three gentlemen in long green coats and tricorne hats, and asked directions for the Queen's house; the men gave them, but seemed to speak distantly, as if they, the visitors from the future, were not there.

On the terrace of the house, they saw a woman with gold-coloured dress and a wide lace collar tucked into it. She seemed to be waiting, with a piece of paper in her hand. In another corner, by a folly, a kiosk which had in fact existed but which had long since been destroyed, they saw a man with thick black coat and a slouch hat and a disagreeable dark scowl to his pockmarked face.

All these things played out in the royal garden as if in mime. The figures seemed to move sluggishly, held back by time. It was only later that it occurred to Moberly and Jourdain that none of the people, or even the buildings and trees, that they saw, were actually contemporary with the busy tourist trap of Versailles and its ice-cream carts.

As the two women compared notes back in England, they began historical research which seemed to confirm what they saw, or felt, was the Queen awaiting the terrible news of the Fall of the Bastille, and the imminent arrival of vengeful revolutionaries who would eventually separate her delicately coiffeured head from her swan-like white neck. The result of many years study resulted in evidence that appeared to be conclusive.

Then, in the rational nineteen-fifties, along came A.J.P. Taylor, in his thick spectacles and his fucking bow tie, to declare in a review in the Observer in 1957 that the whole thing was 'an inflated fantasy by two elderly governesses' (Moberly was fifty-five, Jourdain thirty-seven, at the time of the incident).

This story, the credibility of which was not challenged in my young head, became the subject of obsession to me. The lowering atmosphere, the almost photographic remains of a memory, the darkness of the garden which seemed to vibrate as if liquid in that August afternoon, all struck me as entirely plausible; the way that, around the same time as the women were thrown into a time warp, Paul Nash, as a young boy in London, had discovered an indiscernible place in Kensington Gardens that had no boundaries—only an ancient tree leaning on a metal support like a crutch—yet seemed to him to be 'strangely beautiful and excitingly unsafe', he said, 'more like the sea, whose tides determine its confines, now encroaching, now receding on its shores'. Or the way that in Nicolas Roeg's film of 1976, Thomas Jerome Newton, an alien who has fallen to earth, is being driven through rural New Mexico when he sees a sudden burst of nineteenth-century sharecroppers staring back at him as his limousine drives by.

So too the Versailles garden that Moberly and Jourdain saw and felt, seemed by its own ability to regenerate itself in a simulacrum of what it had originally been, and what it had seen and seemed to be still going on; although all of that substance, all those blooms and seeds and earth and manure had long since been replaced, like Theseus's ship or our own human bodies which entirely replicate themselves every seven years—thereby rendering all of us over seven years old as ghosts of our original selves. That it was perfectly possible that ghosts could grow in a garden's soil, self-seeded in memory, the way that the Edwardian Miss Wilmott scattered seeds of silvery sea holly everywhere she went, all the while keeping a pistol in her handbag for any untoward eventuality as the shadows fell.

I had no grand demesne in which to experience such psychic transitions. The garden to which I was reduced for most of my life in London in the nineteen-eighties and nineties, was the six-foot wide concrete balcony of the ninth-floor of a tower block in Hackney which I occupied, not unlike the walkway of Derek Jarman's flat where he kept bright red pelargoniums as talismanic challenges to the grime of the Charing Cross Road. A defiant act in a world where people like us were told we were not natural ourselves.

The only green place to which I had access was the graveyard where William Blake lay, a man who saw angels in trees and the gender-fluid spirit of John Milton landing in his Sussex garden as if in a scene from *A Matter of Life and Death*. So I grew conker trees in a tub on my balcony as a miniature tribute to William's Albion, where all things begin and end in eternity, with sooty ivy running up a trellis on the tower block wall. I imagined the police helicopter flying by admiring my horticultural attempts as they spied on young offenders racing down the New North Road. I wonder if that balcony is now haunted by my friends stepping out for a fag, by all the parties we threw there, and by the nineteen-twenties cocktail cabinet I'd salvaged from a London Fields junk shop with its let-down mirrored shelf on which to mix drinks and snort drugs while the neighbours knocked on the door to complain about the noise. And I think about this quiet house I am writing in, built in 1921, to which I eventually returned, haunted by the eleven people who once lived in it, at one time, some of whom are still here, some of whom are missing.

The garden is long and narrow and entirely given over to wild life. It's overlong for its site, and threaded with bushes and brambles. Sometimes I don't go down to the end for weeks or even months. I tell friends that there's a Vietnam veteran living down there who doesn't know the war has ended.

There are traces of my attempt to tame the place. I once laid a shingle garden, inspired by Jarman's, in the lee of our creosoted garage whose black lapped boards looked, to me at least, a little like Prospect Cottage. But all that has long since been subsumed. Blackbirds and foxes, slow worms and frogs, hedgerows and pigeons, even the occasional sparrowhawk spying out the sparrows in the giant blackberry hedge which is now nearly as tall as the house.

So overgrown is the garden that only last week I found a twelve-foot high hawthorn tree and a similarly sized sycamore that had appeared without me knowing it. This morning, when I came back from my swim in the inky sea at three a.m., there was a female hedgepig curled up cosily on my doorstep. I apologised as I stepped over her, and her spines shifted a little as she nestled back down. During lockdown, when I thought I might be reduced to digging out a ditch in which to swim if my illicit rides to the sea were foiled by the authorities (at one point I had felt the flash of a camera from a passing police car in the dark), I heard the clatter of hooves in the street as I came home.

At first I thought it was a dog, or even a horse. But it was a roe deer, surreally wandering up the pavement like some Narnian beast. Perhaps she was coming to pay her respects to the skull I'd wrenched from a drowned deer carcass on the beach, and which I had buried in what used to be a flower bed, its horns sticking up like a pruned rose, as if another deer might grow there, rearing up out of the earth, shaking the dirt from its flanks and stalking off down the road.

This ungardened garden, this ribbon of de-reclamation, beckoning in the twilight and dawn, scented in midsummer by jasmine, stinking of fox shit, absorbs all death and life. It keeps on going. Like me. I live on alone in the house, watching through the windows at all the living going on outside. I expect a passing deer to press its arse to the glass, the way kids do to the underwater observation port at the local baths. I wait each year for the leggy pelargoniums to reach up to the sky in my rackety conservatory, where I used to lie naked as a teenager, sun bathing in the open doorway when everyone was out, and which itself is so overgrown now that it resembles an aquarium.

There's a plaster shell there, painted turquoise and gold, salvaged from the garden at Wilsford Manor, where the Honourable Stephen Tennant grew old, waiting for his tropical lizards and birds to creep in out of the winter cold, while decorative straw hats still rested on the banisters of the arts and crafts staircase for Lytton or dear Siegfried or Baby to wear. They'd dressed up in floral chintz outfits to re-enact their own fête champêtre by the slow-flowing Avon.

It was 1927. I might have seen their thin and willowy ghosts there, being filmed all the while by a tall young footman in dark glasses. I remember Stephen's hand as he shook mine, and the autumn wind shaking the front door downstairs, blowing leaves in from the garden where baroque statues had long since tumbled into a tangled carpet of ivy and bamboo.

It was a place utterly removed from my experience, so far away from my life that it might have been a dream. The madness of it all, the decadence, the vanishing century, my suburban self standing there, briefly in that story for one moment. I realised that every garden is a time machine and we are the ghosts. And I look at my bones now, and how they have grown, and the flesh that has blossomed from them over the years like a reef, and I am grateful for this fertile soil from which I came, and the dust to which I will return.

Philip Hoare

Ana Mendieta
Imágen de Yágul, Mexico, 1973

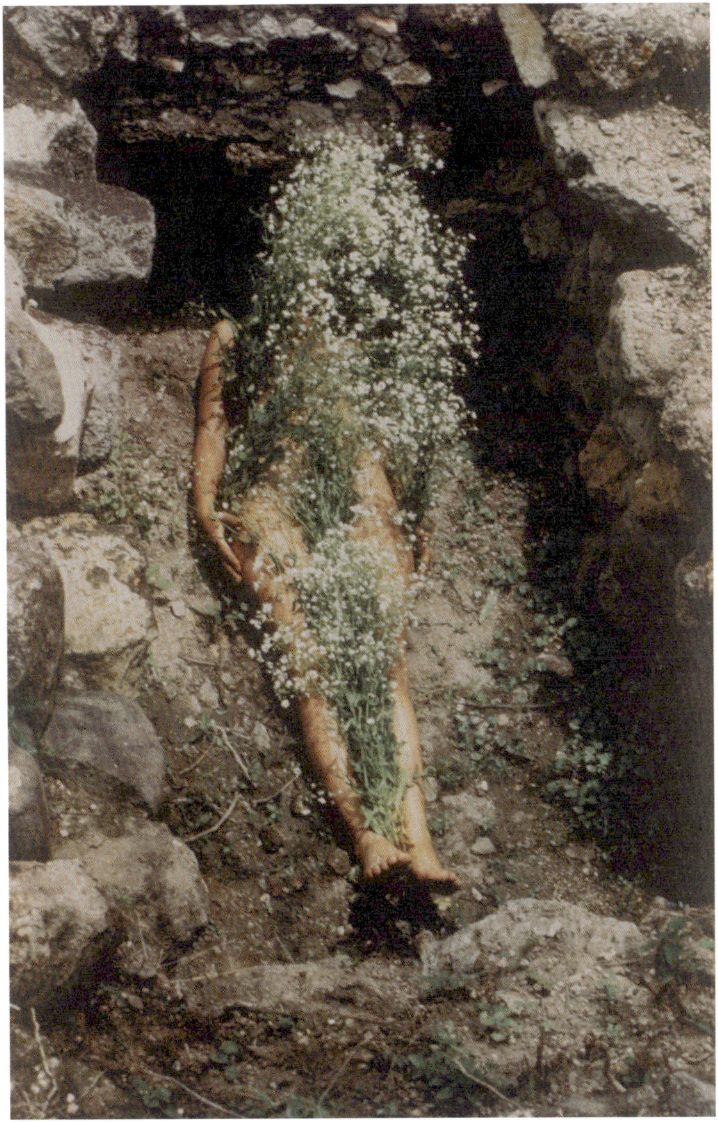

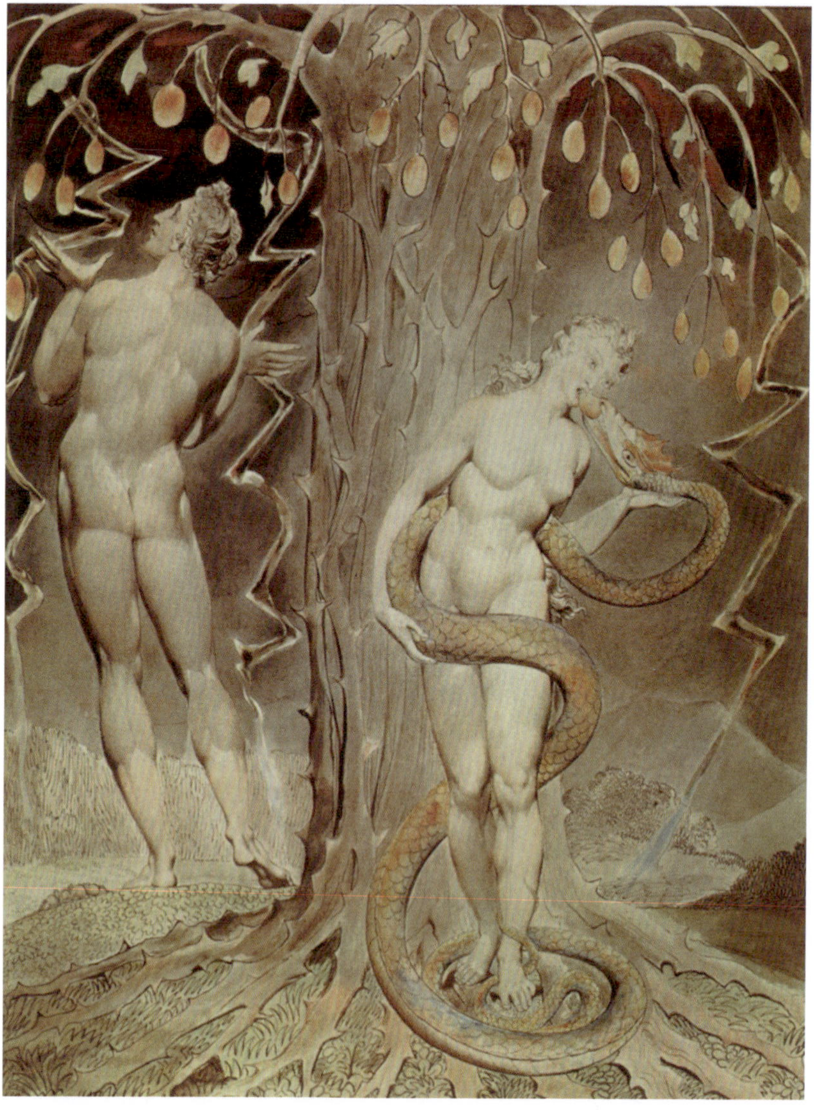

William Blake
The Temptation and Fall of Eve, 1808
Illustration for Milton's *Paradise Lost*

SEED COLLECTING
Yellow Rattle
Ragged Robin
Foxgloves
Cowslip
Verbascum
TO DO LIST
CANAL ROPE
Thyme Garden
Meadows
MOW GRASSES
Pond
Terrace
Field Studies Council guides to plants/meadows

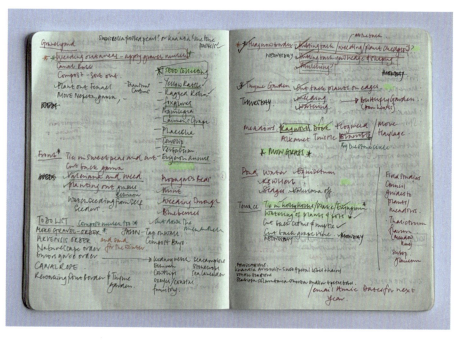

Letter to the Future

Dear Gardener,

I want to give you a seed box containing seeds from 3 different plants to begin a wild garden of your own. Seeds are ideas; infinite beginnings; time travellers; living historical artefacts; and mysterious magical life-starters. They are sourdough yeasts for soil, the basis of all that can grow.

To garden with seeds is to shun the "instant garden": the garden as a product. Seeds reveal that true gardeners are those that work with the dynamic processes of life and immerse themselves in a world that transmutes time into a cyclical spiral. The seeded garden is a realm where human need and imagination co-creates with plant. This is a world our intrinsic selves know well but the Anthropocene is blind to.

Within a self-sown seed is held all the microbial intelligence of the parent plants. The relationships that sustain a plant within your garden's specific soil biome are encoded within that seed. When seeds make contact with soil they recognise the life held within the soil as kin. Sugar exchanges from the germinating seed are reciprocated with inputs of water and minerals that allow root structures (part plant, part fungi, part bacteria) to grow. These seeds I am giving you contain community, immunity and a plant's best chance of enduring a changing climate.

The seeds come from a garden meadow that grows on the ballast, rubble substrate left behind on a railway line that once ran through what is now our garden. Meadows and long grass have always been a motif of the wilder garden. Gardening rebels like William Robinson and Christopher Lloyd have used them to reject the conservative conventions of the tightly mown lawn and poke fun at the uptight, bio-phobic character of a more orthodox controlled horticulture. Wild gardeners like Pam Lewis have cultivated them to blend the garden into a gentle mix of human aesthetic and nature reserve. Pioneers such as John Little sow them to demonstrate the need for a new dynamic garden that integrates nature connection and habitat into the everyday human landscape. You can use them to foster your own garden relationship. But please be aware that these are seeds from autonomous 'wild' plants – they cannot be curtailed or controlled.

The first seed is the seed of the field scabious, a limestone meadow plant that flowers from late June into October. The field scabious has a pale lilac pincushion flower that dances high above the meadow grasses on wiry hairy stems. In a meadow they are elegant, in an herbaceous border they grow too large and flop awkwardly. Field scabious like dry, nutrient poor soils and take time to establish. Field scabious used to be a ubiquitous plant in the southwest of England but their populations have declined as farming and land use have intensified.

There are an estimated 270 species of bee native to the UK and approximately 250 of them are solitary bees that don't live in colonies or hives. The honeybee is the only farmed bee and often out-competes solitary bees as a result. Native solitary bees have co-evolved with native wildflowers, and some are solely dependent on a single or small number of indigenous plant food. *Andrea hattorfiana*, the Scabious Mining Bee is, as its name suggests, dependent on the field scabious. The female can be identified as having a shiny black abdomen and laden with bright pink pollen from the scabious. She will need at least 72 field scabious flowers within a 900m range of her chosen fragment of sandy poorly vegetated soil in which she can burrow her nest to provision her eggs with pollen. Somehow, within ten years, this bee is now visiting our garden meadow, resisting the declining trend.

SOW SEEDS IN MEADOWS!
Yellow Rattle
Cowslip
Knautia
Fritillary
Campion
Geranium
Hornbeam hedge
Stone Cairns

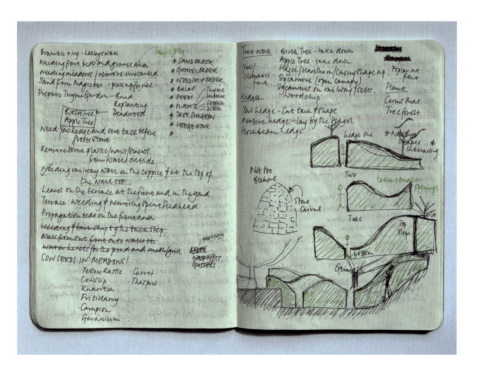

Gardening with plants that are vernacular to place feeds a deep belonging. It gives refuge to wild species that are increasingly threatened by changes in habitat, farming and climate change. It bonds us to the small, the local, those that we share space with. It explains garden ecology as a delicate web of inter-relatedness and co-dependency. It nurtures a noticing and an adaptation of our own gardening practice: moving from the controlling hand to one that fosters inclusion and collaboration. It shifts us to notice the wild plants that exist in the overlooked fragments of railway sidings, brownfields, and roadside verges and recognise these scraps as valuable relics of rich plant communities that sustain life.

Hedge Shapes
One
Two
Three
Top slope
To Buy
Electric hedge trimmer (small)
Kneeler
Waterproof
Waterproof trousers.
Small Electric leaf blower
Electric Strimmer
NEXT YEAR
Mow the meadow bank (knapweed) until April/May
Euonymus planipes
Acer campestre - deciduous (from plants)
Taxus baccata (Yew)
Cotoneaster 5m x 5m 'Rothschildianus'
Malus
Hazel

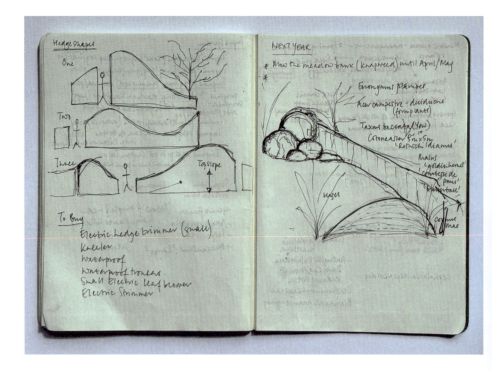

The second seed is the seed of the bee orchid. The bee orchid is fascinating, it mimics a female bee in scent, texture and appearance to lure in a male to attempt to mate and, in so doing, pollinate the orchid. The bee orchid is also self-pollinating. Bee orchids like dry limestone grasslands. Unlike other orchids, they are most likely to be found near human disturbance: industrial sites, roadsides, lawns, parks, quarries, gravel pits and soil heaps. They prosper in the mess we leave behind us and are one of many reasons why brownfield sites are often ecologically richer than farmed countryside.

Orchids are mysterious beings. Most seeds come prepacked with protein to enable the embryonic plant to grow. Orchid seed is like dust, it has no protein energy reserves but can travel large distances. Germination can only occur where certain mycorrhizal life exists in the soil to provide the seed with the nutrients to germinate. This relationship between orchid and fungi allows orchids to survive in some of the most inhospitable places where other plants would struggle.

Orchids choose the garden, rather than the gardener choosing the orchid. The gardens that they choose foster soil relations by banning chemicals, allowing wild grassland edge communities to grow and avoiding fertilisers. The gardener they choose is one that understands gardening as a practice that primarily cultivates soil health so that the microbial life can better cultivate the plants. In the orchid-strewn garden the gardener recognises that soil and plant have been interacting and interrelating for 700 million years, the gardener's understanding of the work they are doing is limited and truncated. Our best bet is to give them as many opportunities as possible to grow.

The third seed is that of the meadow maker plant, the hemi-parasite yellow rattle. So many gardeners are making meadows that the seed of this plant is now highly sought after. Yellow rattle lives on the root systems of other plants, particularly grasses, depleting their vigour and opening the sward to allow wildflowers the space to compete. An annual plant that has to set seed or be sown every year, the seed needs a period of chilling over winter to be able to germinate. In our meadow a relationship has become apparent between the badgers, who like to scrape the railway line for grubs on frosty nights and successful germination.

Yellow rattle is an arable weed: poisonous to livestock and depleting the 'hay crop'. Our relationship with yellow rattle, as with so many of our wild plants, is a history of swinging between two poles of high regard and dislike. Our binary ways of ordering, parasite/mutualist; wild/human; weed/flower; native/invasive alien; pest/wildlife, are absurdly useless in the wild garden. This is why gardens can expand the human mind and cultivate us. Gardens are the liminal space between human and other, between parasite and reciprocal, between us and them. Boundaries and edges soften and blur, plants travel and evolve. You can either police the boundaries of the garden and be forever thwarted, or you can allow the horizon in.

There is a widely held assumption that man-made meadows and grasslands have always been places for grazing animals. But they are much more culturally significant than this. They are communities of plants that have co-evolved with us – medicinal herbs, dye plants, plants for food, plants as cultural history and plants for use. Many wildflower communities are sustained by a reciprocal stewardship with humans that has been overlooked to both our detriment. Reclaiming this relationship and integrating it into a more progressive, ecologically informed, welcoming garden is vital to us and the life that sustains us.

My seeds come to you without the obligation for you to reciprocate, but, with the understanding that an honourable harvest passes its riches onto the next generation. Seeds can only be 'saved' by growing them on into plants and allowing them to reproduce through open pollination. They cannot be squirreled away in a bank vault as a possession. They command their own gift economy.

Once your plants mature and set seed you are beholden to pass the gift onto others. Seed gifting is the gentle way that we transform the garden into fertile ground for resilience, resistance and change.

Dear Gardener, please keep sowing the change.

xxx

Jo McKerr

Tabboo!
Disable Comments, 2018
Acrylic on paper

Courtesy of Gordon Robichaux and Karma

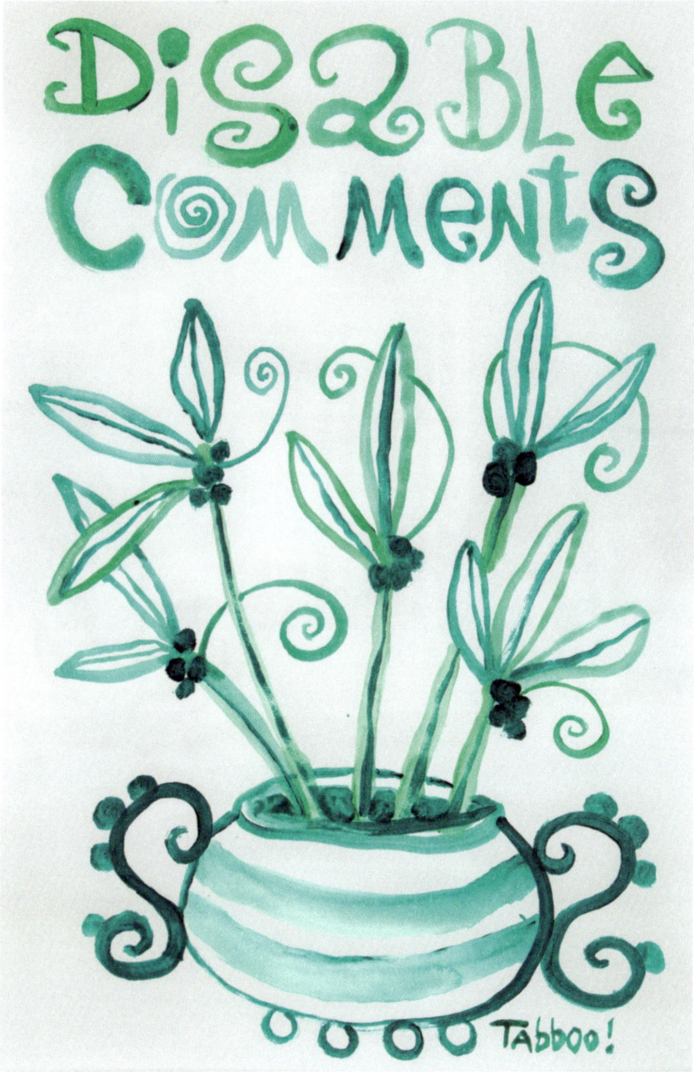
DISABLE
COMMENTS
TABBOO!

56

Elisabeth Kley
Trees in Uzbekistan, **2019**
Glazed earthenware

Courtesy of Canada Gallery

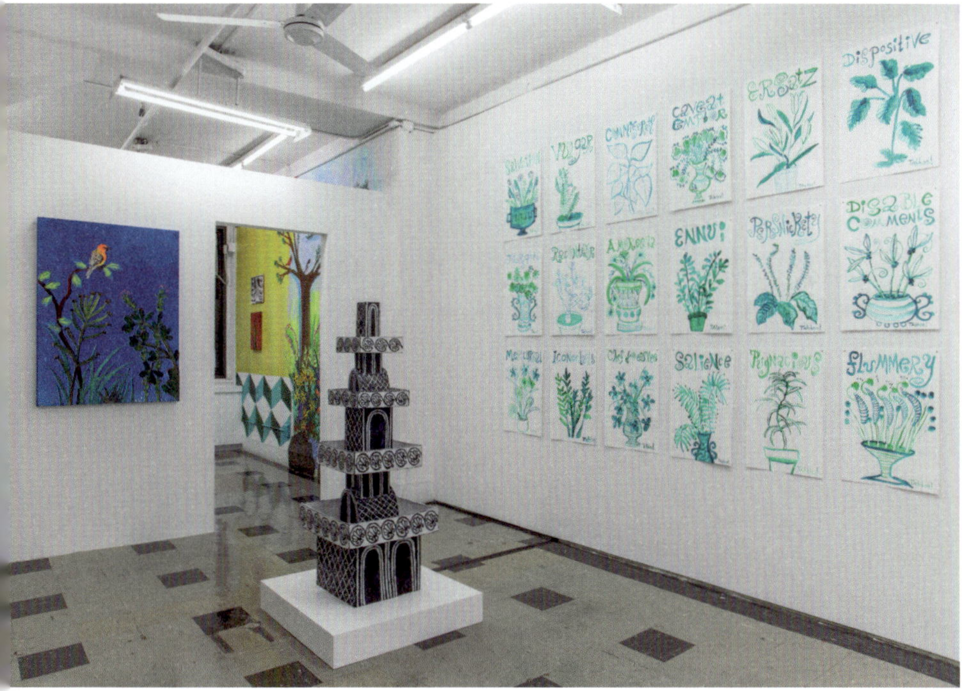
Dispositive
ERSATZ
ENNUi
fluMMERY

Installation views of *Garden*, 2019
by Elisabeth Kley and Tabboo!

Courtesy of Gordon Robichaux

Palestinian Heirloom Seed Library

Heirloom seeds also tell us stories, connect us to our ancestral roots, remind us of meals our families once made at special times of the year. The Palestine Heirloom Seed Library (PHSL) is an attempt to recover these ancient seeds and their stories and put them back into people's hands. The PHSL is an interactive art and agriculture project that aims to provide a conversation for people to exchange seeds and knowledge, and to tell the stories of food and agriculture that may have been buried away and waiting to sprout like a seed. It is also a place where visitors may feel inspired by the seed as a subversive rebel, of and for the people, traveling across borders and checkpoints to defy the violence of the landscape while reclaiming life and presence.

Founded by Vivien Sansour, the PHSL and its Traveling Kitchen project seek to preserve and promote heritage and threatened seed varieties, traditional Palestinian farming practices, and the cultural stories and identities associated with them. Based in the village of Battir, a UNESCO World Heritage site outside Bethlehem, the PHSL also serves as a space for collaborations with artists, poets, writers, journalists, and other members to showcase and promote their talents and work. Working closely with farmers, Sansour has identified key seed varieties and food crops that are threatened with extinction and would provide the best opportunities to inspire local farmers and community members to actively preserve their bioculture and recuperate their local landscape.

The PHSL is part of the global conversation about biocultural heritage. Its Traveling Kitchen is a mobile venue for social engagement in different communities, promoting cultural preservation through food choices.

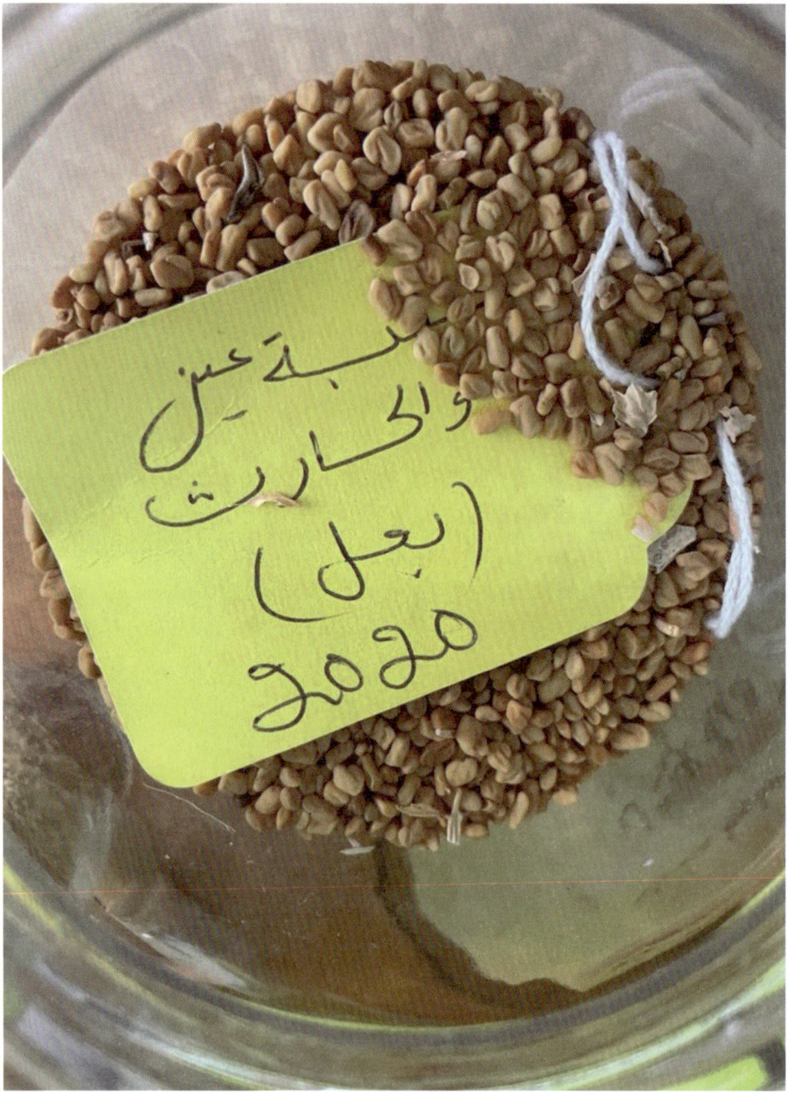
(بعل)
2020

جليج اليقطون

TANGLE BELONGING

Name it alert sense flight now
        in a sentence of excess
luminous state unroll plunge blossom
        end wake in sight of
bee bits of after stumble true or in
        full flower beneath a
sunny simple matter for handling depth
        thought light in the words:
edges planted to vanish or locate lines
        composed on water
seen as newt flash wren song shaking
        left a leaf quite different
frees seeds sinks and last green stem
        on the other hand for
use in high time sent on as it ages
        for fungal outlier change and so on.

Ian Patterson

We harvested the seeds from this enormous project at Heligan in Cornwall. That's Jamie's OVA symbol 100m across. We held eight rituals through the year (Beltane, Summer Solstice, Lammas, Autumn Equinox etc) with all sorts of local groups like kids with SEN. We then took the harvested seeds to places like the site of the H Block prison at Long Kesh in Belfast. Spread a little magic in a desolate place…

— John Marchant on Jamie Reid

Photograph by Cian Smyth

Jamie Reid

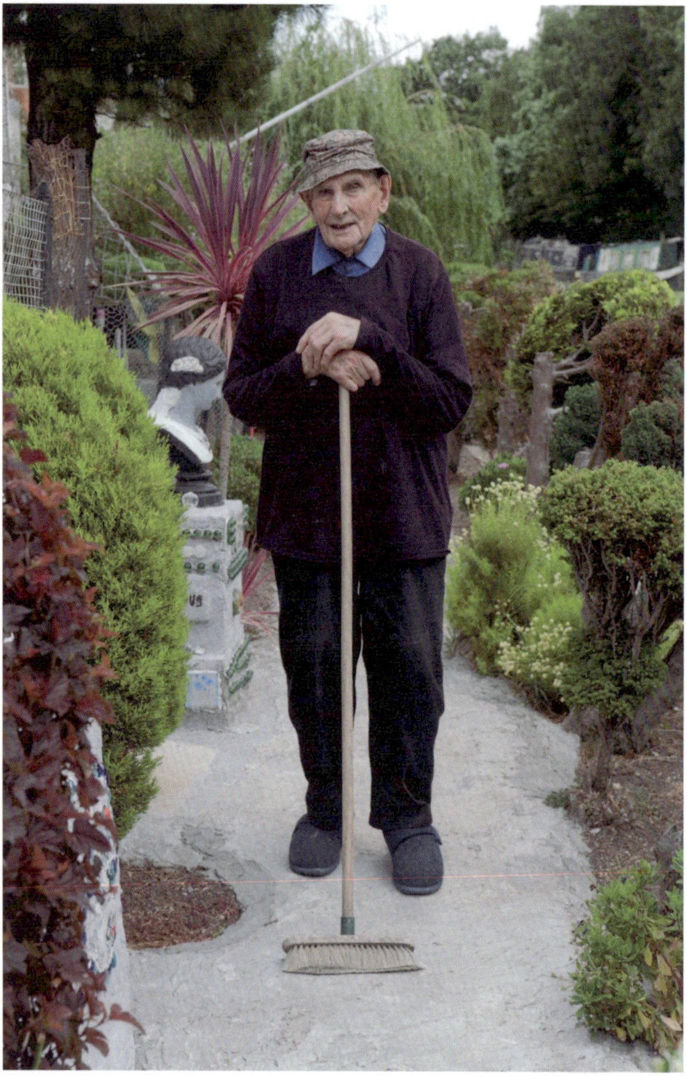

Gerry's Pompeii

'96 I think I made my first statue... I kept continuing statues after that... I wanted to do a lot of statues... Go out and make more, you know. That continued on and on until nearly I had a hundred statues. 115 I got now... But then the garden of course – the garden was wild when first I moved round here, especially along the canal. It was covered with beds, bottles and everything else there. Took me about 6 months to clear it... First I planted the trees, the conifers round the edge. Then I planted the others – Llewellyn or something – conifers. I planted a pine tree down the bottom which is fairly tall. My sister brought that from America... I'm planting flowers at the moment. The sculpture of me? Gerry the Gardener. I'll cut his head off I think. No, it's a failure. Don't look like me, but some people say it's alright. Maybe it's the way you look when you are 90... I never thought I would do so much, but I did do. In the days before television we didn't have much to do so we had to devote our minds to something else. One thing is it kept me off the streets. They'll be astonished what they'll find in my garden in years to come. It'll be like Pompeii or something – Gerry's Pompeii.

— Gerry Dalton in conversation with Roc Sandford, 2014

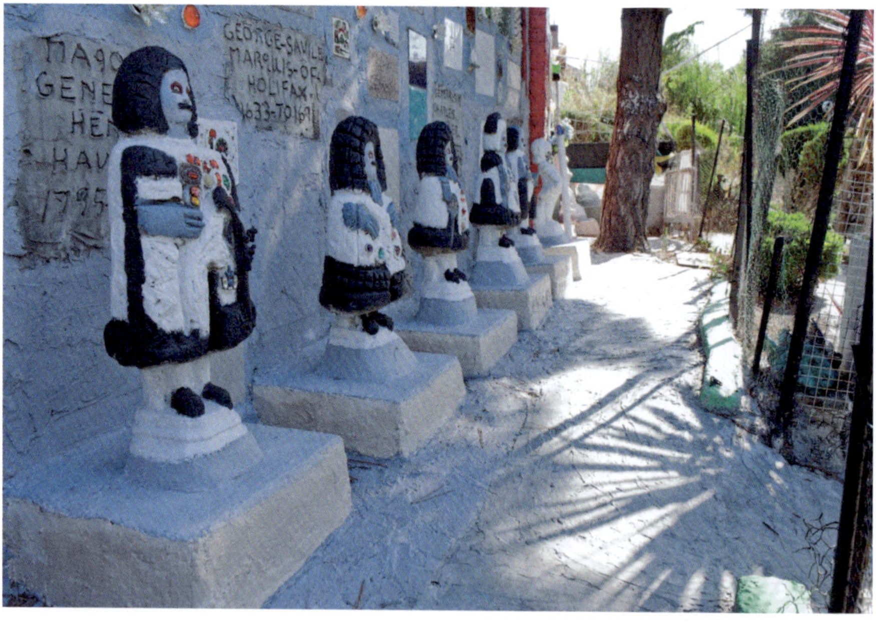
GEORGE-SAVILE
MARQUIS-OF
HOLIFAX
1633-7016?

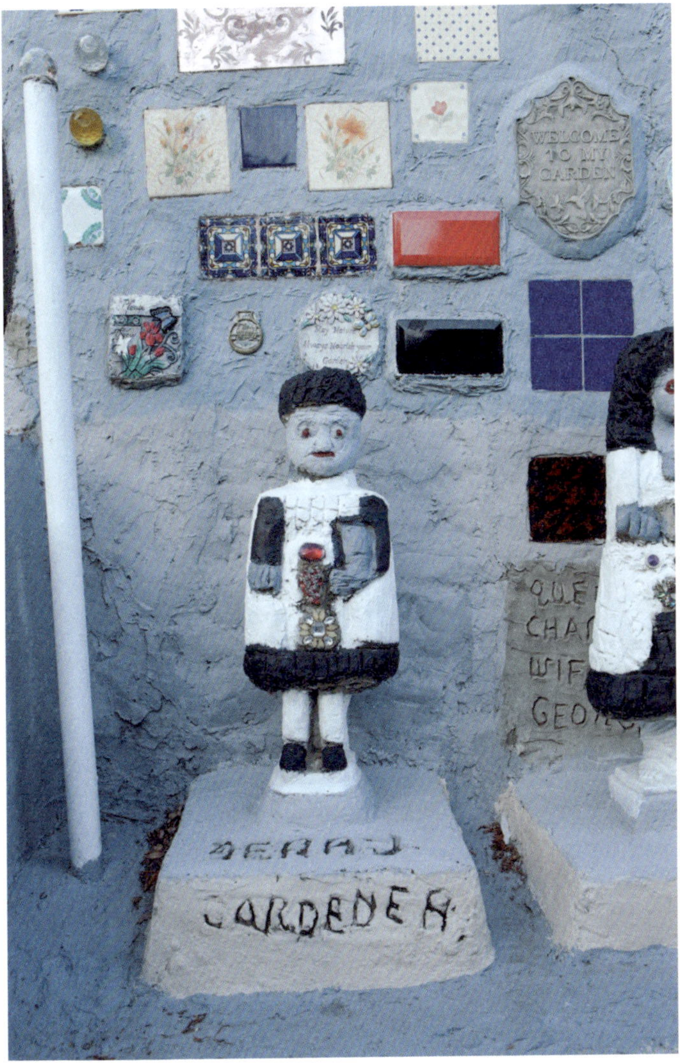
WELCOME
TO MY
GARDEN

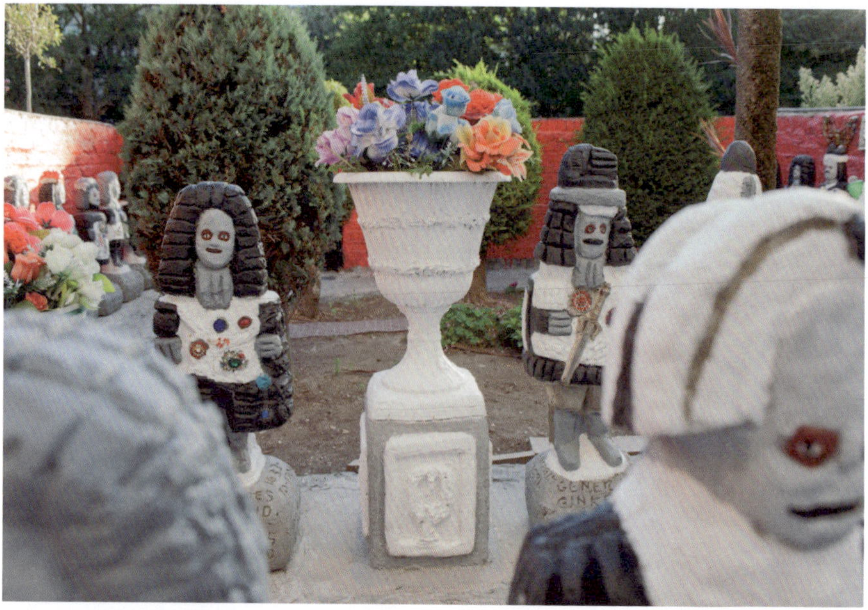

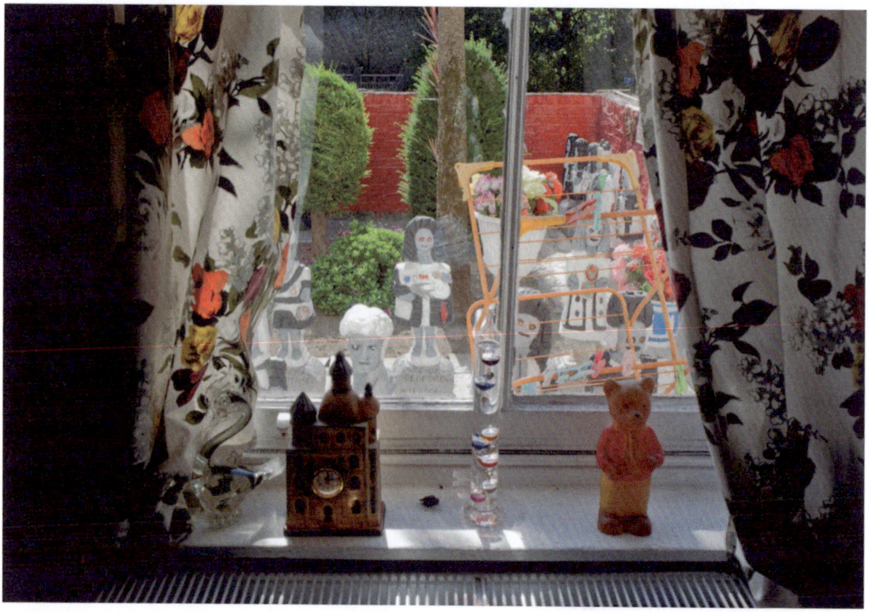

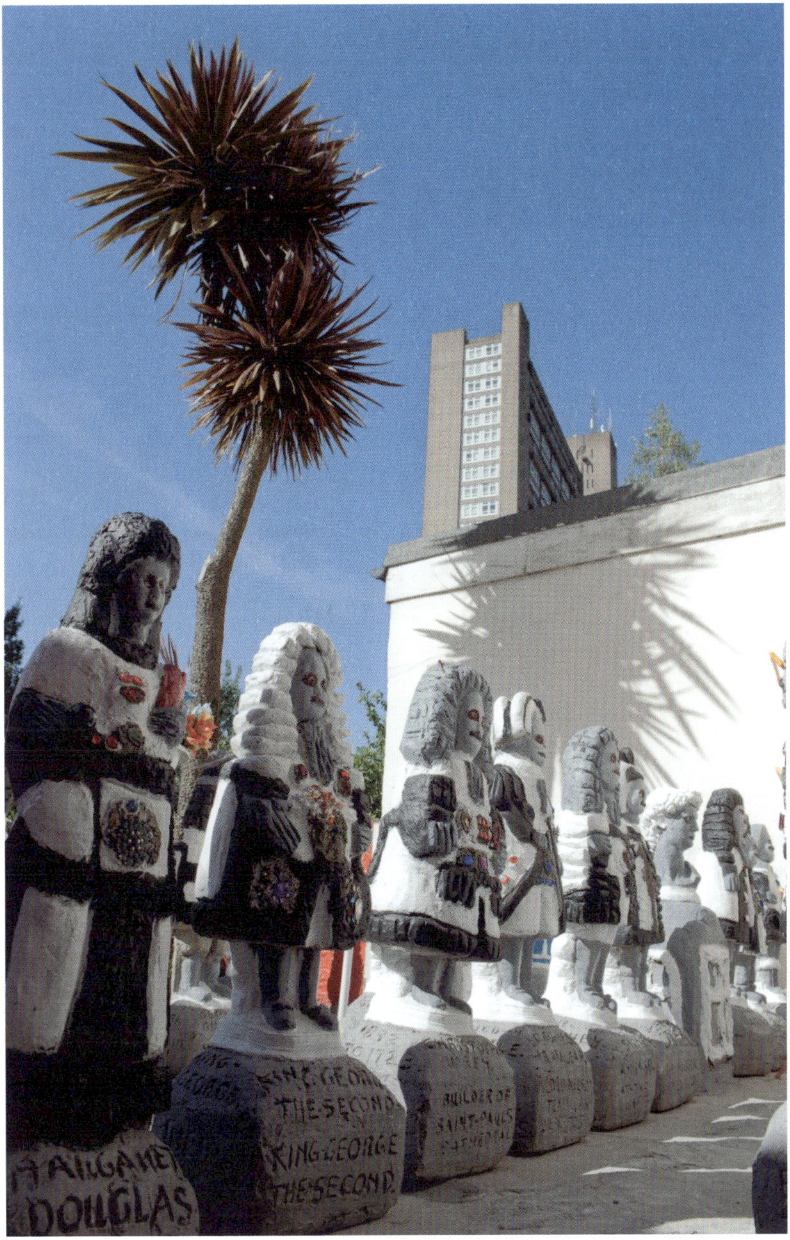
THE SECOND
KING GEORGE
THE SECOND
DOUGLAS

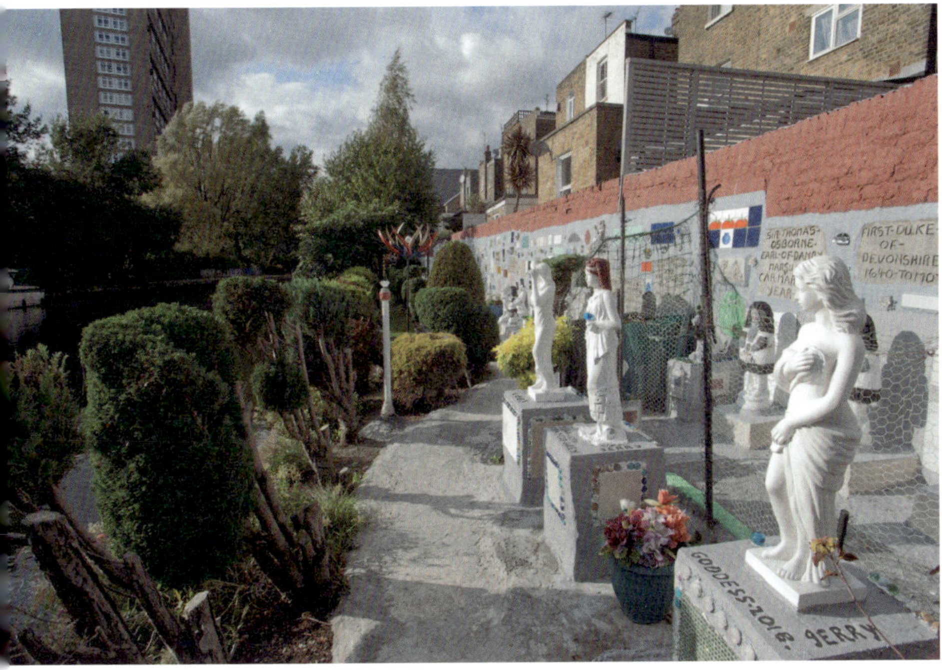
SIR-THOMAS-
OSBORNE-
FIRST-DUKE-
OF-
DEVONSHIRE
GODDESS-2016. GERRY

Gerry Dalton
Photographs by Jill Mead

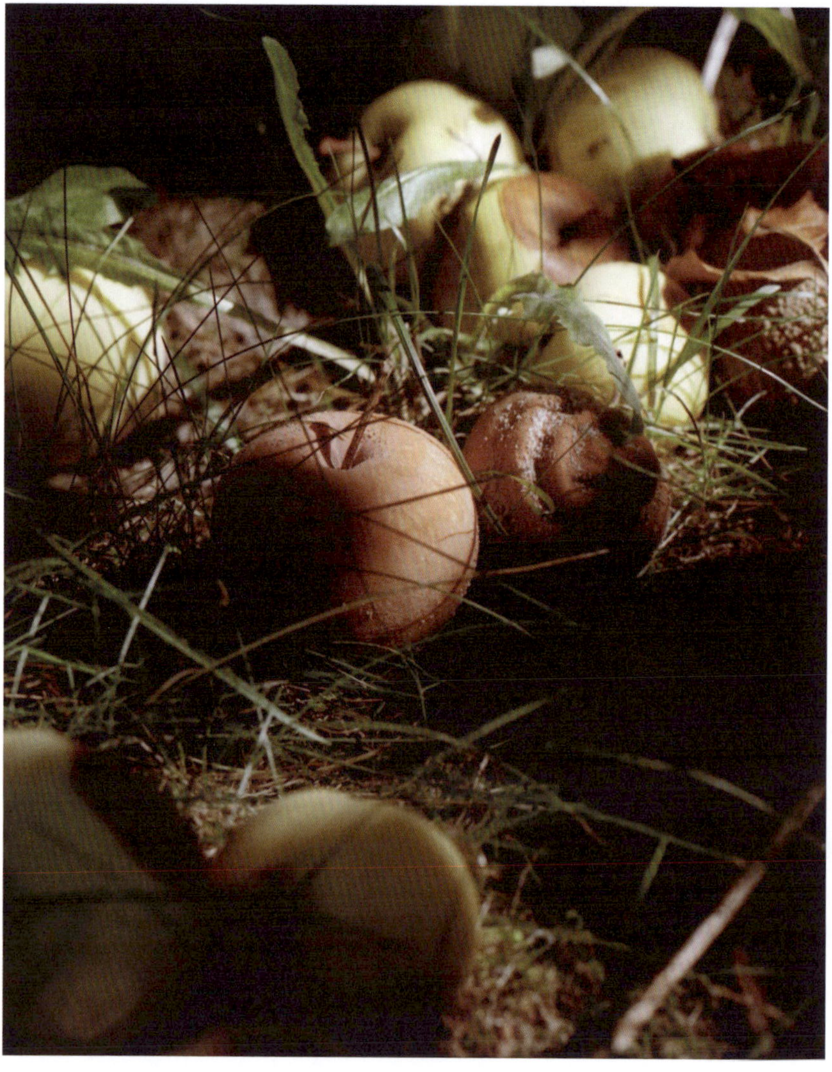

My late grandma's garden of the fallen apples. The paper apple, Papierówki, is a special type of tree that has apples every other year and grows mainly in the Eastern Europe region.

Kuba Ryniewicz

A Childhood Garden

The Tay leaps into view, revealed when the train takes a sudden turn from Fife onto the ancient railway bridge, and alongside, the sleek length of a more modern road bridge crossing the vast estuary of the Tay River into Dundee and onwards into Angus. It is a sight that never tires, rich still with adventure and nostalgia woven into memories that flood back, a constant in my early years, remaining so even now in later life.

Then again, that familiar thrill that can never be stilled as the journey continues inland to a small village outside Dundee. The approach to the Kirkton of Auchterhouse is on the rise of a hill sloping gently towards the Sidlaw hills, and beyond, reaching further north to the Grampians, to the west is the stretch of the Cairngorms and in the distance the perfectly angled peak of Schiehallion.

Fragments of memory come to mind, turning into a drive through a gap in the trees along the roadside, down what had once been, when I was just a few months old, a path mown through a small field of wheat, to a house newly built by Mum and Dad, shaped like a block of cheese dropped from the skies, a curious new shiny sibling, and quite as boisterous.

Ah Mum and Dad, what magical ambitions they realised. Eschewing a life in town to raise a family in the country with ne'er a boundary in sight and realise a cherished dream, a garden.

There were shelves of Mum's cookery books throughout the house and to match them, Dad's books on gardening in all manner of shape and form, often open at photographs and illustrations of acers and elegantly planted maples and rocks alongside photographs of rocks and rills in a Scottish landscape all with scraps of scribbled on paper and notes.

Being on a rise, behind the house and the few others mostly tucked away behind trees, fields became moorland rife with tangled heather sloping gently towards Auchterhouse Hill, the only hill among many with a summit stuck with trees that survived the wild winds blowing in from the North Sea.

Mum and Dad enjoyed life at a gentle pace and time moved slowly in our new home and plans and change happened over the years as we grew. The field of wheat was slowly replaced by Dad's imagining of a garden and the levelling of soil dug for a driveway that had for gates, railings from our school in Dundee, and the foundations of the house were carefully placed in mounds upon which was built a terrace with steps made from yet more rocks from local quarries, now so forbidden and protected, and pebbles, brought from holidays on the Hebrides.

Another terrace looked onto pools and waterfalls through trees, ferns and rocks. Dad was never one for half measures, and I can just recall the gargantuan cranes and JCBs in the driveway and the excavations and placing of huge rocks and boulders that he had sketched in a quarry and then had lifted and transported to be placed just as in the drawings made of those parts of the garden hidden from view except from the house.

As we grew in our fiefdom, Dad wanted only plants and trees, growing flowers in one bed only. Outside my window, it was home to an elegant, prettily scented yellow rose from Mum's childhood in India that bloomed each summer and was cut with care for a vase on the dining table. Beside the rose was a fantastic peony the colour of a cardinal's robe that was nicknamed Richlieu from the piles of adventure books by Dumas and Baroness Orczy, creators of so many characters that peopled the imagination of a small boy, with a mind as fertile as the garden.

The beds planted at either end of the house led to stretches of grass surrounding the walls that supported the terrace built around the house. All around were placed plants and trees along with ferns of many sorts.

There were a few herbs planted and a solitary rhubarb, the oddly few vegetables and fruit grown, as rare as flowers throughout the garden. The densely planted parts leading to the front of the house were wild in contrast to a more considered planting around the house, along the terrace, among the steps and all around and behind the falls and pools.

In winter, among the plants, a few flowers grew such as Mum's beloved hellebores or, as we knew them, winter roses, and snowdrops, so cherished and so loved, flowering in clumps all through the garden and carefully cut for only a few pretty glasses on tables inside. Daffodils appeared and were politely admired. Crocuses had appeal only on the banks of the road leading up towards the hill but given short shrift, for no apparent reason I can recall, when found growing in the garden.

There were little pink blooms on bushes here and there, but mostly the colours were greens of every kind on every tree and plant in summer leaf. Until, that is, technicolour exploded from a raucous summertime of rhododendrons, azalea and clematis grown wild, as blousy and playful as the titles for My Fair Lady, for not only was the garden a lifelong adventure and passion of Dad's, the idyll was an enduring gift for his wife, our Mum.

Mum was in the garden often, always in summer time, be it for podding peas, hulling strawberries, hanging washing and laying tables outside, or a flurry of blankets for a picnic. All this while Dad cavorted with some new-fangled, labour-saving device for lopping off branches too high to reach or a natty grass cutter that would end up in a rather ugly garage along with all the other discarded notions.

The garden of my childhood was light, bright and spacious with lawns, not quite yet swallowed by the spread of conifers, acers, beech trees, ferns, hostas and hellebores that Dad planted with glee, caring little for borders and, heaven forfend, anything remotely ordered. If there was any neatness, it was usually due to a youthful sapling requiring space to be planted.

The spirits of the garden ran as free as us kids. And when play was suspended, as the sun shone upon the quiet of a warm day settling on the garden, cushions and rugs, pillows and blankets were heaped on grass and reading vied with napping while butterflies danced in a hushed stillness, the only sound, that of water falling off rocks into pools, an occasional bee and, now and again, a page being turned on a book.

A childhood summer flowered like the blooms of that season. Our holidays on the Hebrides saw us leave behind a garden becalmed and gentle, and on our return we were greeted by grasses waist high and weeds unchecked in proliferation and we bolted from cars with sand still in our shoes to explore the new wilds. There was a drill of sorts to reclaim the garden and as Mum pinned load after load of washing on the drying lines, the quiet was rent by the sound of a grass cutter and the gathering of weeds by the basket load with us all returning the garden to something of its old self for the last days of summer and holidays.

As summer waned with the fanfare of golds and reds of autumn, the carefully planted acers along small paths along with all the other trees and plants turned from summer's abundance to their splendid autumn livery. And all the while, we cavorted or read in our little realm, caring not for much, for our needs were few and well met by Ma and Pa. And when I walk along a path, beside the low walls of the terrace which were once the ramparts of our youth, I smile at the thought of how small as children we once were.

Autumn saw our return to school and the garden became a distant place as we left early for school returning as the sun began its descent and we were despatched to our rooms for the ritual puzzlements of homework, looking out of our windows onto a garden already shivering as the temperatures lessened and the winds returned.

Winters of my youth were bitingly cold and the ground iron hard with a frost worthy of a Dulac illustration and snow that would swallow you whole when leapt upon. The garden took on the garb of mystery, as did the land, trees in stark silhouette, branches wine dark with damp, and when the snows fell in wild storms and flurries, one could easily conjure faeries, silkies and broonies and ponder what thoughts were sowed in the mind of JM Barrie who was born up the way in Kirriemuir.

No longer with us, the passage of years was required to walk in the garden once more and smile with only the memories of Mum and Dad at our sides. The spreading ferns, hellebores and hostas thrive still beneath huge overblown conifers and rhododendrons, banks of azaleas and clematis grown wild and let run to the top of the highest trees be they pines, larch or maples, shadowing pools and rocks that echoed far away lands woven into the rills and wilds of Scotland.

In bloom, the colours of so much planted to illuminate the garden with the joy, laughter and humour of Mum and Dad with plants from the highlands, rare blooms from the Himalayas woven with a serenity of gardens in Japan so beloved by them both.

When walking through the garden, Dad would spout plans for a particular spot along with the Latin names for the plants found, which his keen mind amassed. He had a great appetite for all manner of subjects that fed his many interests and persistent curiosity. No detail was ever missed, regardless of how wild the garden became, as some parts grew with great enthusiasm. Dad would pass such exuberance by with barely a look but would instead sometimes pause by a tree with a bright moss on the trunks, just to notice and comment, with a gentle pride, that this was a sure sign that the soft, gentle air in the garden was clean and pure.

And now, where light once danced in water, still flowing when bidden, reflecting the skies, the often stilled pools are green with growth, imparting a mantle of quiet and secrecy as if cloaking the palimpsest of a dormant dream: a garden untended around a house mostly shuttered and closed until those times my sister returns.

A new generation flings wide the curtains, opens the windows once more on a garden matured, and youthful voices are heard again in the wild and overgrown garden created by Mum and Dad that once was our playground. The plants, bushes and trees are grown tall from reaching for the sun, having to grow in the shadow of older trees that were once a simple palisade, barely the height of a child, enclosing our home in a deep quiet, now become, with little restraint, a wild wood.

Jeremy Lee

Lubaina Himid
Inside Out - tiled wall for a back yard, 2024

Courtesy of the artist

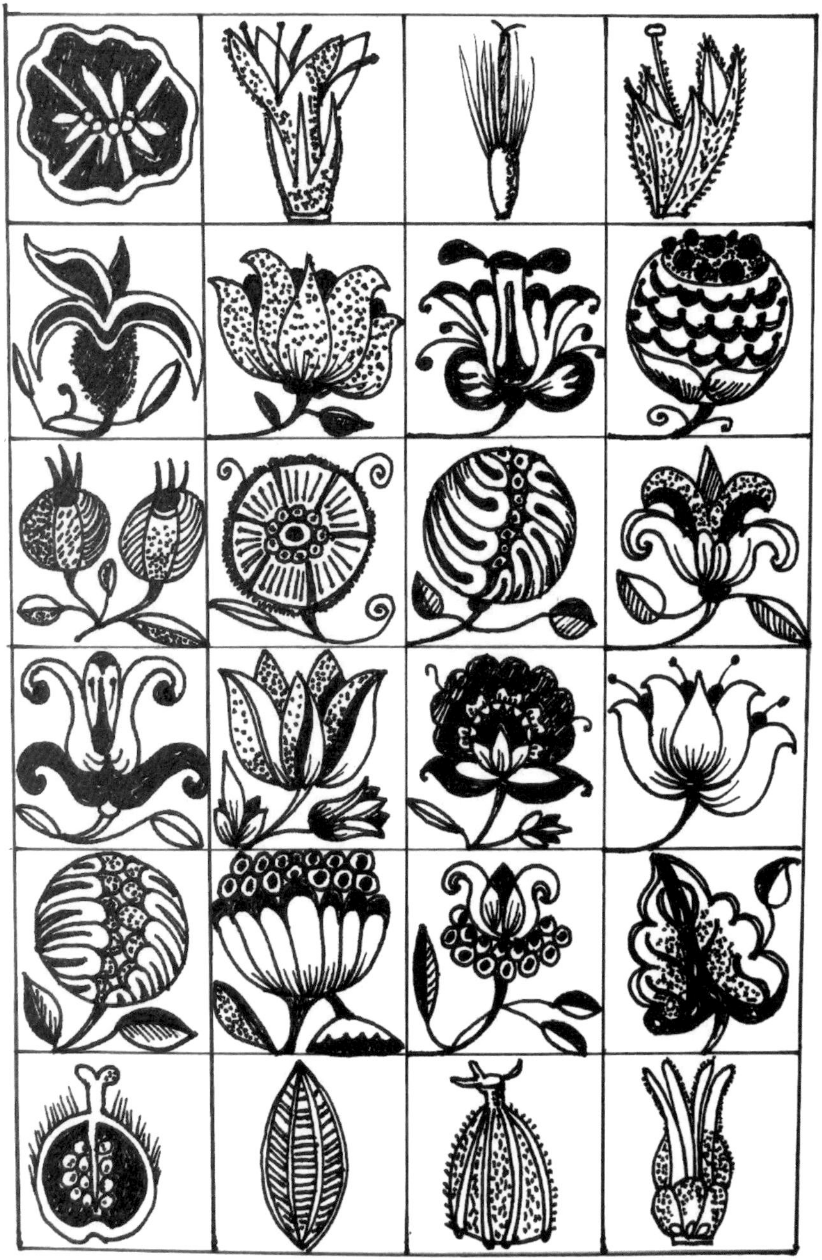

Here

The wish to garden: a wish for plenitude. The practice of gardening: a confrontation with failure, a crash-course in disappointment. Like psycho-analysis, a return from grandiosity and wish-fulfilment to the limitations of reality, a painful, painfully necessary descent. What I want is an intact bio-sphere. What I want is total sensory immersion, a world beyond me, to participate in a communal Eden that is everywhere and all at once. Big dreams. Decades of longing. What I get is what the gardener always gets: small triumphs, myriad disaster, constant emotional richness. Add to this the 21st century's ceaseless soundtrack of chickens coming home to roost. Microplastics, poison in the water, poison in the air, everything implicated no matter what innocent intentions you had for it. I've been reading my diaries from my twenties, my sad, self-scourging diaries. They're punctuated with pages torn from old newspapers and National Geographics. A photo of alliums, a photo of Derek Jarman blind and sorrowful in his hospital bed, his pyjamas the colour of buttermilk with navy-blue piping. The garden was his answer to multiple catastrophes. AIDS, homophobia, Thatcher, capitalism, greed: make a garden as a spell for unwinding time, for starting again with changed priorities. I took it to heart. In every diary, I find plants. Notes on actions, plans for an affinity group called Nettles, our finest hour setting up a front room outside McDonalds, complete with standard lamps and sofas, and serving baffled shoppers free cake and tea. For which outrage I was banned from McDonalds for life. That was my favourite kind of direct action: garden-style, prodigal and not for profit. Herbaceous borders for the people, as luxuriant as a stately home but do it in a wasteground or a public park. I was training as a herbalist, spending stray afternoons sitting in the Wild Park or deep in Kingley Vale, drawing toadflax, trailing St John's wort, selfheal, ground ivy, ribwort plantain, learning to see the intricacy of any common place. The devastation of the AIDS years had given way to the devastation of planetary destruction, encapsulated in Britain by an un-bridled programme of road building set in motion by the Major government in the 1990s. I remember being in a friend's flat in Brighton when we heard that the protest camp at Fairmile in Devon was being evicted. I cried with shame that night, to be part of a species that could destroy somewhere so beautiful, its circle of ancient oaks so vast you felt almost spooked to see them. Like shooting elephants. That reckless, that degraded. Sometimes I travel down the A30 now, but I can never pinpoint the place. It's been nowhereised, turned into backdrop from the window of a car. For a long time the book that became *The Garden Against Time* had the working title *Here*. A garden is a way to be in place, in right relation to other lives, and the desire for a garden, I still think, is a desire to return not to the Eden of the Bible but to the true and heretical Eden, which is a communist state for every living being, everyone entwining and humming with life. You can't find that at the Chelsea Flower Show, but I see glimpses of it everywhere I look. Hawksbit in the abandoned pub next door, glowing in the late light. The clematis my neighbour, ninety-three, has woven through his gate. Living on terms with other creatures, being a participant and not a king. When I say I like to garden I mean I like to dream continuously of a better world. And then I like – but maybe you do too? – to be prodigal, to broadcast the living seed.

Olivia Laing
Great Dixter, Summer Solstice

The Romance of the Closed System

In the early 1990s, a countercultural group called the Synergists built a miniature replica of the planet. They called their geodesic marvel Biosphere 2 because planet earth, they explained, is Biosphere 1. Inside the hermetically sealed earth laboratory was a small rainforest, an ocean with a living coral reef, agricultural fields for food production, a desert garden, and savanna grasslands.

The Synergists wanted Biosphere 2 to be a test run for sustainable life on Mars, so they recruited eight "biospherians" to live fully-enclosed inside the terrarium for two years.

The science fiction novelty of the project attracted media fanfare. Two years later, when the biospherians left their mechanical eden – rife with in-fighting, oxygen deprivation, and hunger – they were largely mocked and derided as a cultish spectacle.

I made a film about Biosphere 2 called Spaceship Earth, and while filming, I became close with one of the biospherians named Linda Leigh. Today Linda lives in the small Arizona town of Oracle where Biosphere 2 still stands as an open-air university laboratory and tourist attraction.

When I met with Linda in Oracle, she went through her shed looking for old photographs, videotapes, and documents to share with me for the film. I came home with a stack of audio cassettes, which I discovered were sessions that Linda recorded with a dream therapist during her enclosure.

Linda was surprised she still had the recordings, and she gave me permission to use her hours of reflections, observations, and fantasies from inside the closed system.

October 23, 1992

Linda Leigh: What's happening out there in the big world?

Dream Therapist: I would say the odds are 3 to 1 that Clinton has it. So that's happening on the political level. The economics are in a malaise still. The feeling that nothing is really going to change is very much in the air.

LL: Yeah, I've been thinking about the processes here. The process of cycling elements is very fast, and it seems that everything is speeded up… Emergence of a culture is speeding up, and probably personal transformations are speeding up too.

DT: Why do you think?

LL: Hm, God, I think that there's probably a lot of things. One is that we don't have so much input from the outside. There's so much noise from the outside, just with the modern civilization that I normally live in. To be in here is to be encapsulated and protected from a lot. There's not all this noise, so there's more attention to internal things.

This latest dream I had was inside the biosphere and it was in the rainforest. It was mostly this mountain that we have at the center of the rainforest, which is very dark gray volcanic rock.

There was a lot of rumbling and movement in the rocks, and it was a volcano that was clearly going to erupt. So I started to slowly climb down the mountain, and then I saw a man running down the mountain from the top, who I didn't know. There were these boulders flying through the air and rolling off people's backs, but I never got hit by one. Then after the eruption, I went back to the base of the mountain, and there was this primordial ooze. As I looked, new species that had never been in the biosphere before emerged from the primordial soup. I just sat there and stared at them with awe and delight.

DT: So what I experience talking to you and working with your dreams is a woman with quite extraordinary capacity and empowerment, which has been directed in the first part of your life into a very kind of – how can I put it – orderly kind of way. Your curiosity is now stronger than your ability to deny or avoid it.

LL: I think I said this last week... Dreamtime, like asleep dreamtime, and awake time are merging very closely.

November 12, 1992

The other day, Jane Goodall came and looked at us through the glass. I've never been observed by somebody who is really a master observer, but I felt the way a chimp must have felt being observed by her. It was lovely – there was no judgement, no strange wrinkling of the nose, or curiosity in that way. I guess intrigue is what I'm thinking of. It was really grand to be on the other end of this profound observer.

And there was another person there, a man named S, who somehow I got a real hit from. And he started talking about dreams and asking us about dreams. I felt a real, really extraordinary contact with him, like he was going to be a playmate type of thing. You know, when you see somebody and you think, oh, this person's going to be a friend. It turns out he worked for 30 years with Joseph Campbell.

And so I talked with him on the phone the night before last, and he said he felt quite a great energy coming from me and that there were shamanistic qualities to it. He thought that I was the one person in here who is really alive.

He identified me also as a friend, and he thinks that we should develop our friendship over the phone. I agreed, and it was really extraordinary to me.

June 11, 1992

I would have brought in food a long time ago for people, and everybody knows that I would have because I think that in order to keep our workload up that we should have kept our strength up.

We humans are co-evolved with plants, and we're symbionts. We have to have them. They have to have us. We need to take care of each other – there's no doubt about that. There's no question about that whatsoever, but here I am, 14 pounds lighter, and where have those 14 pounds gone? And, altogether, biospherians have lost probably about 210 pounds, which is equivalent to two more biospherians. So, the biosphere has eaten two biospherians. Is it parasitic? What is the relationship now between the biosphere and the biospherians?

I think a lot of things are sacrificed here for the romance of the closed system. Sending out for pizza is not romantic.

So it really feels like being a pioneer. You know, the more you physically suffer, I think the more it reinforces the romance.

December 14, 1992

I've been having wonderful talks with S on the phone, and that's been really swell, super, excellent, wonderful, delightful, all of those things. What's really happening is we're deciding what we do with the relationship we have over the telephone and will later have in person. And it's interesting that both of us seem to have, at the same time, come to a place where we feel like it's time to be relational and make that kind of the primary thing.

We're talking about just anything under the sun, including past relations, things that are our dreams and our visions, and what each of us wants to do. I guess I get confused about how to deal with the fact that it's only over the telephone, and that's part of the frustration. I've been writing, not only talking, but writing letters to S and faxing them to him. My writing gets really, really good when I have a focus for it. Even though my writing is normally a lot about plants, you know, it really comes out when I have a focus for – when I have a person to focus on.

That's what I'm trying to figure out – just looking in terms of the definitions – what is eroticism, really? Maybe it's looking at the mystery of interconnectedness. And that connectedness, for me at least, is with the whole world of life. It's through plants.

And now, that connectedness has a focus in love for a human being. And so, somehow, and I'm not really sure how it all kind of fits together in terms of definitions, I'm having both a really strong link with the world of life, and also now with a person.

Whenever I have one of these long talks with S, I just kind of stay awake for hours at night thinking about it, and so I end up getting really really tired.

December 23, 1992

I had an extraordinary dream last night. Everything just kind of flowed into each other. I heard some Shinto ritual music. Then I went into the savannah, and I just started weeping. It just came out like the fears and sorrows and grief of the world was pouring out of me. It was astounding – tears were spewing out of my eyes. I was at the corner of the savannah and the agricultural area, and I could see that there was rain coming in from outside, and it was raining on me on the inside as I was crying. Then a galago – they're like our primate pets here – came down within a couple of feet of me and started screaming at me because it didn't know what was going on. I think he was really scared, but I wasn't scared at all because, you know, this thing was happening, and it was exactly what I'd wanted to explore. It was a release of all of this grief that I've been carrying around. Then, I went further into the savannah, and vines reached up to me and started entangling my arms, and I started seeing that anywhere I would touch. These vines were circling my arms, and I was looking way over into the rainforest and feeling that there was a circuitry between the energy I was putting into the plants and all the corners of the biosphere. We were all connected.

July 6, 1993 (2 months before re-entry)

I'm now recalling that I have a personal relationship with every single plant in the rainforest, in the savanna, in the desert, either having touched it because I collected it or grew it or I sectioned it or photographed it, planted it, propagated it. And not only that personal relationship with every plant, but also with justifying why it should be in here in the first place, the species lists. What good is it in a biosphere? What part does every plant in here play in the biosphere? Justify, justify, justify, at least for myself, if for nobody else. So, I sit surrounded by Boswellia carteri, scratching the under pedals of Boswellia carteri, thinking about how Bos got here and what care I took with Bos in order to make him grow. Quite a story.

It's all part of the intensity of being in this closed system.

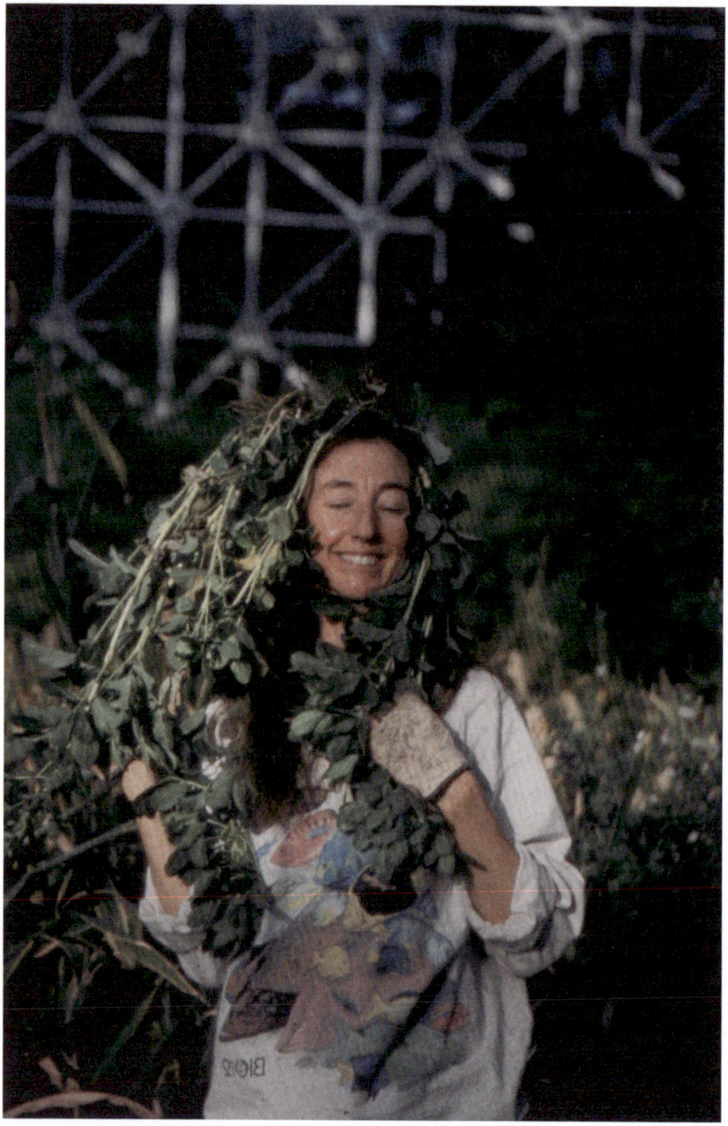

Matt Wolf

103

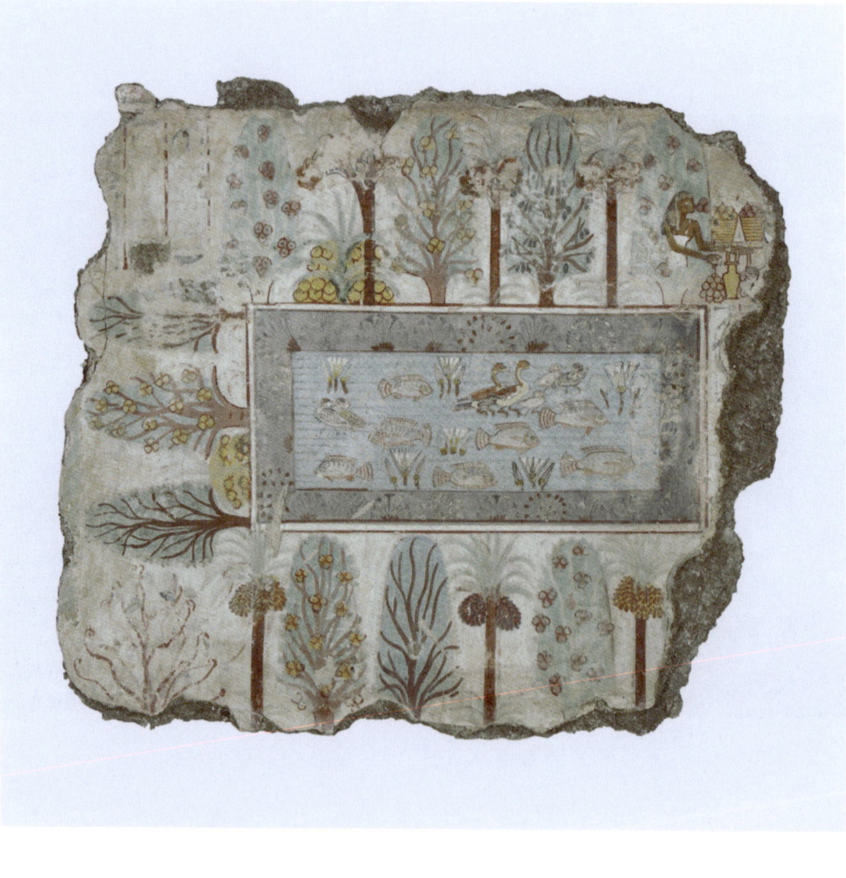

Unknown artist
Fragment of a tomb-painting from Nebamun's
estate garden, c.1350BC, Egypt

© The Trustees of the British Museum

Scott Treleaven

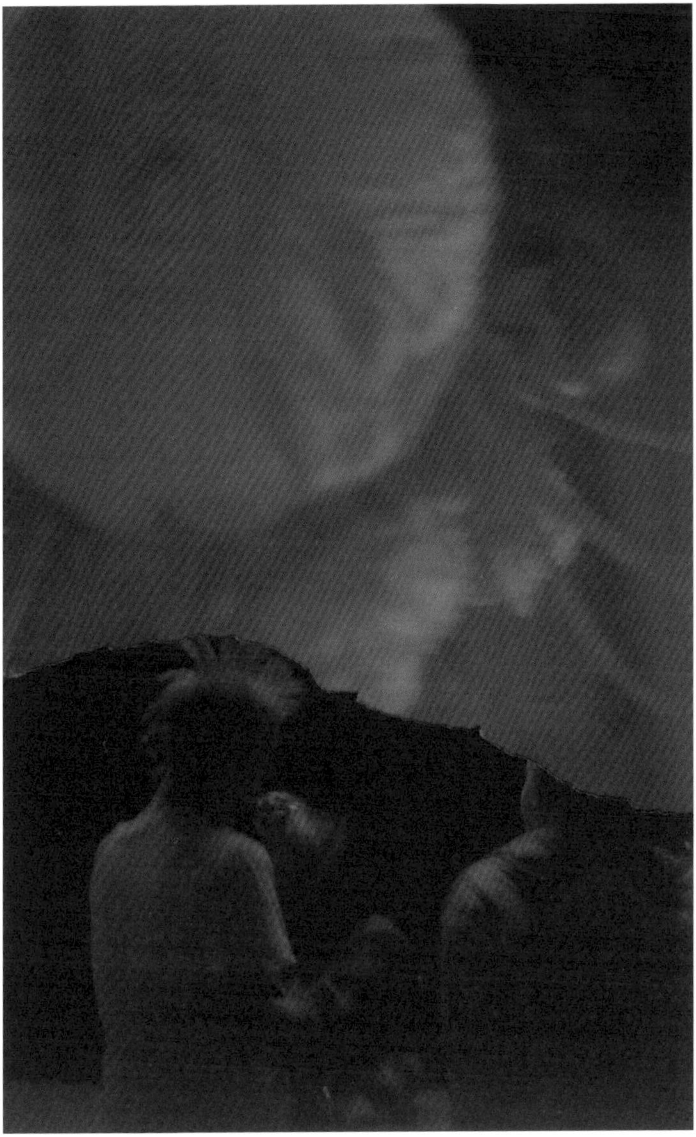

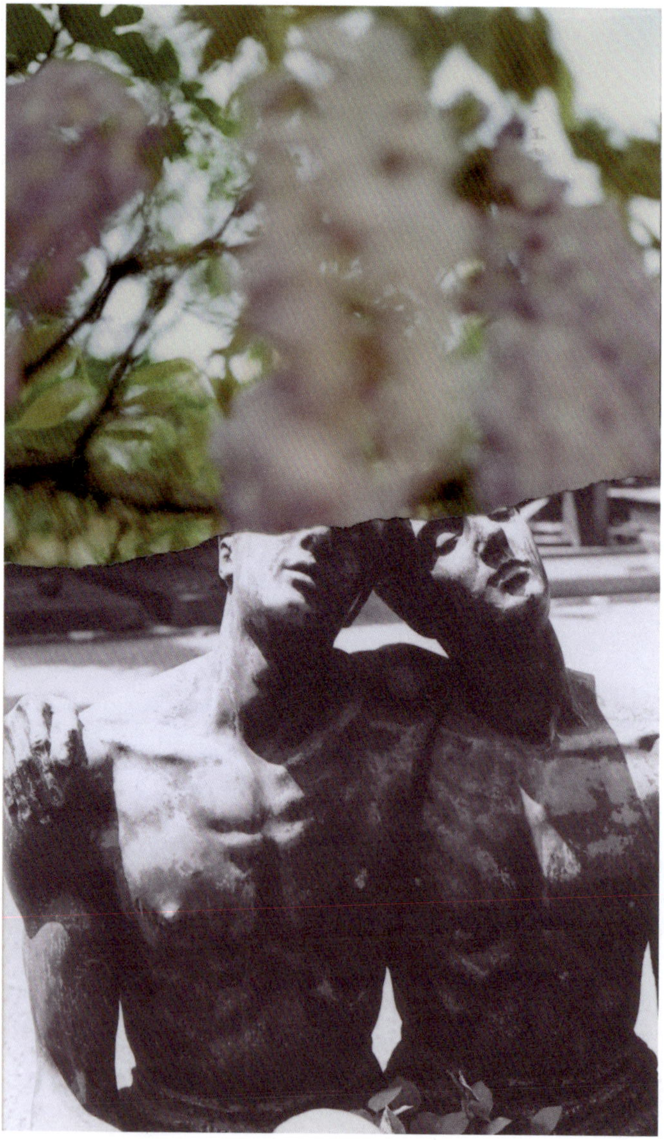

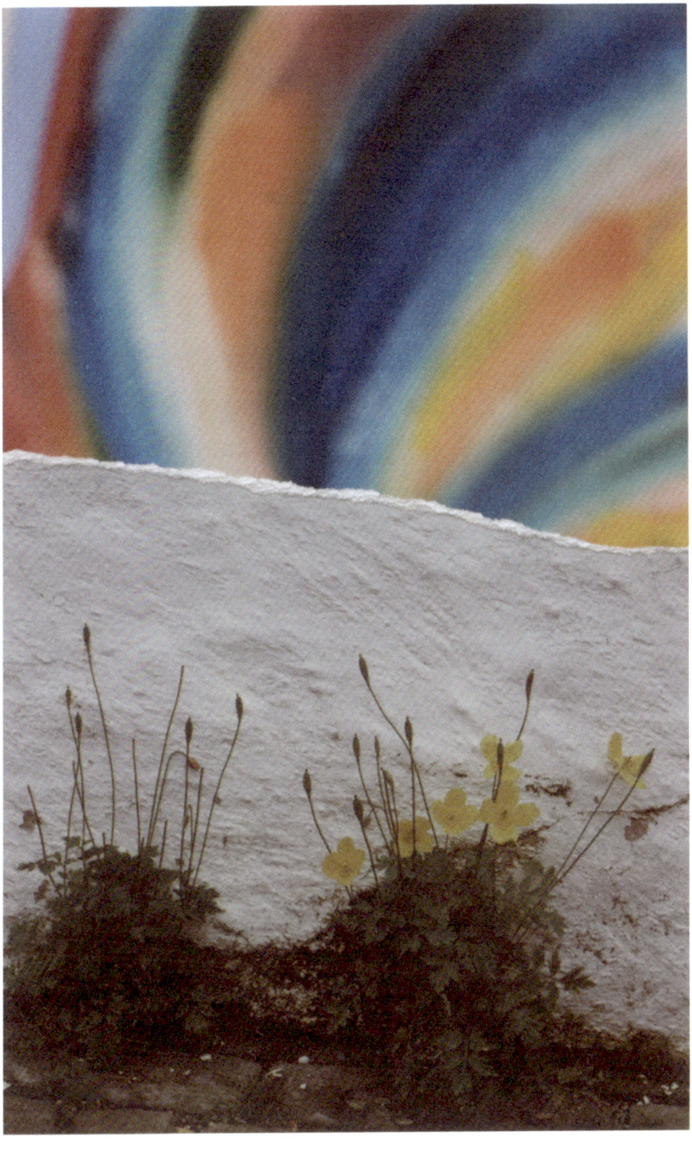

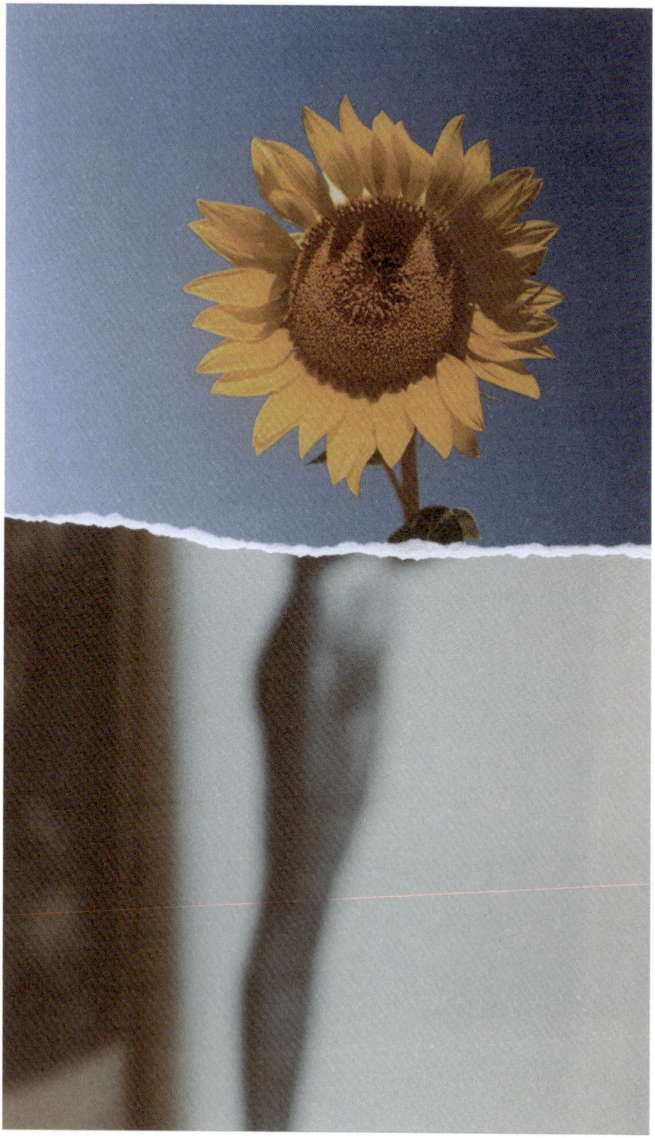

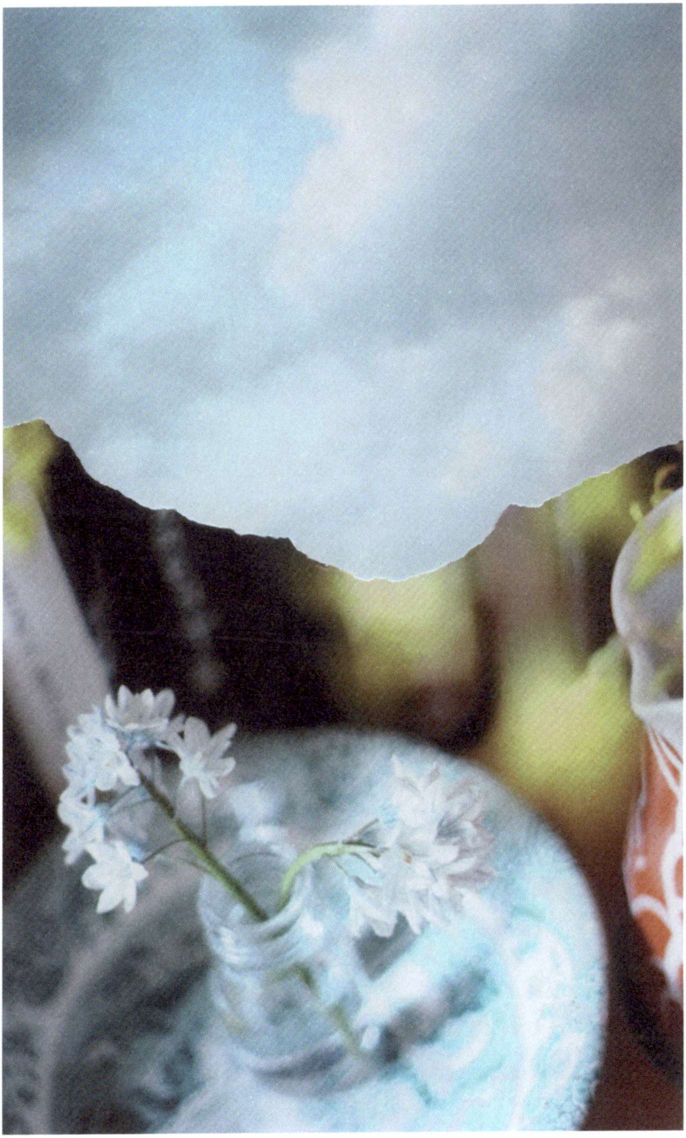

1. *Untitled (bouquet, Paris / drunk friends, San Francisco queercore show, 1990s)* **2022**
Photocollage from artist's 35mm negative prints

2. *Untitled (wisteria/Cimitero Monumentale, Milan)* **2024**
Photocollage from artist's 35mm negative prints

3. *Untitled (unfinished painting/Bergen, Norway)* **2023**
Photocollage from artist's 35mm negative prints

4. *Untitled (sunflower, Toronto/sculpture, book page)* **2023**
Photocollage from artist's 35mm negative prints

5. *Untitled (sky, location forgotten/striped squill, Toronto)* **2017**
Photocollage from artist's 35mm negative prints

Courtesy of the artist

The Devil's Rope

Indigenous Americans would call barbed wire 'the devil's rope' for the way it would ensnare the buffalos who, while searching for water or land to graze, couldn't see it well enough to avoid it. They would die, trapped and left thirsty and starving, their torn skin bloodied.

A tool of settler colonialism, it was created to swiftly partition the vast plains of America's midwest. The settlers couldn't wait for thorny shrubs to grow along the newly formed boundaries of the stolen land they were impatiently, hungrily laying claim to so enlisted barbed wire into their branch of the colonial project.

Now, a few hundred years later, this brutal creation has been rendered benign – ordinary, even – through the ubiquity of carceral logic and private land ownership, and the threat of violence they rely upon.

Private land, after all, is not a natural nor inevitable occurrence despite how impossible it can be to imagine a world freed from it. All lands were once common, a shared inheritance. Now barbed wire scars our landscape to keep us from what is ours.

Yet, day after day, with my hands in the soil, I let myself imagine a world without barbed wire. Where land is accessible to all and the landscape is open to holding our hungry desire to repair our disrupted relationship with the ecosystem. Imagine the gardens we could grow!

While I harvest leafy greens, little spiders in my hair, I let myself imagine the discovery of some plant or organism capable of bioremediation that, like the fungi that can heal contaminated ground, could soften and dissolve the spikes put in place to tear at fur and flesh.

And from there, what other possibilities might grow?

Maybe a composting of the fences that keep us from one another?
Or a shrugging off of limiting identities that impede our cross-pollination?
Perhaps a creeping, scrambling, vining, rooting, tearing down of the boundary walls that embody the arbitrary, man-made, ideological nature of borders as we follow the path of our plant kin towards verdurous liberation?

Imagine the gardens we could grow!

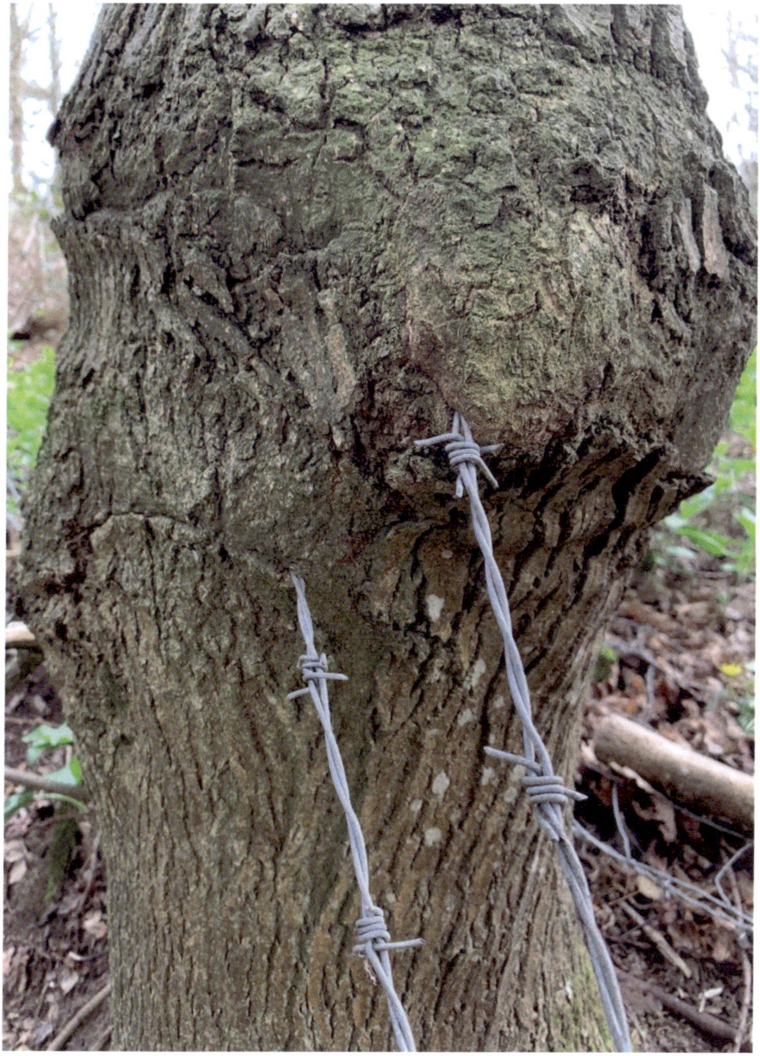

Claire Ratinon

Touching Green

I entered a dialogue with the natural world when I began to garden as a child. The simple act of tending and observing, responding and being in process very soon became second nature. Something I chose to do over most other things and, as the years went by, now do for it being the place I feel grounded or, very literally, earthed.

The more I participate in the silent conversation, the more the liminal places on the edge of the discipline have become the draw. The wilder parts where the lightest of interventions deepen an understanding of where we fit in. A wet fold in the land here at Hillside, which we call The Ditch, is a place where the horsetail and twisting bindweed have the upper hand and where we have to be subservient as gardeners. Taming this place would be out of the question, for it is certain we are no longer the protagonist, but finding a way to be part of it means we are drawn here to bear witness to its domain and order.

A mown path, which narrows as the season grows, allows us a better opportunity for what my friend Midori refers to as 'touching green'. Led by the natural order, we see where the niches might be and how the plants choose where they want to be. Where the springs make the ground constantly wet and the marsh marigolds thrive. Where the shadow from the willow cools in the afternoon and the lushest foliage is most comfortable.

The *Rosa soulieana* and the elecampane are strong enough here if given a yoke of clear ground for a couple of years to help them establish. Enough time to rise above the competition and then become part of it, as we are for keeping the watch. A gentle steer to favour the primrose over the bramble that once hid the run of water. Then making way for wild angelica and a proliferation of meadowsweet and marsh thistle. The year upon year observation is a slow but sure process of getting to know. A deepening knowledge of when to step in and when to stand back and simply listen.

Dan Pearson

Huw Morgan

This is a drawing I did of the pots in the sun room at Prospect Cottage the year that Keith Collins, Derek Jarman's partner, died.

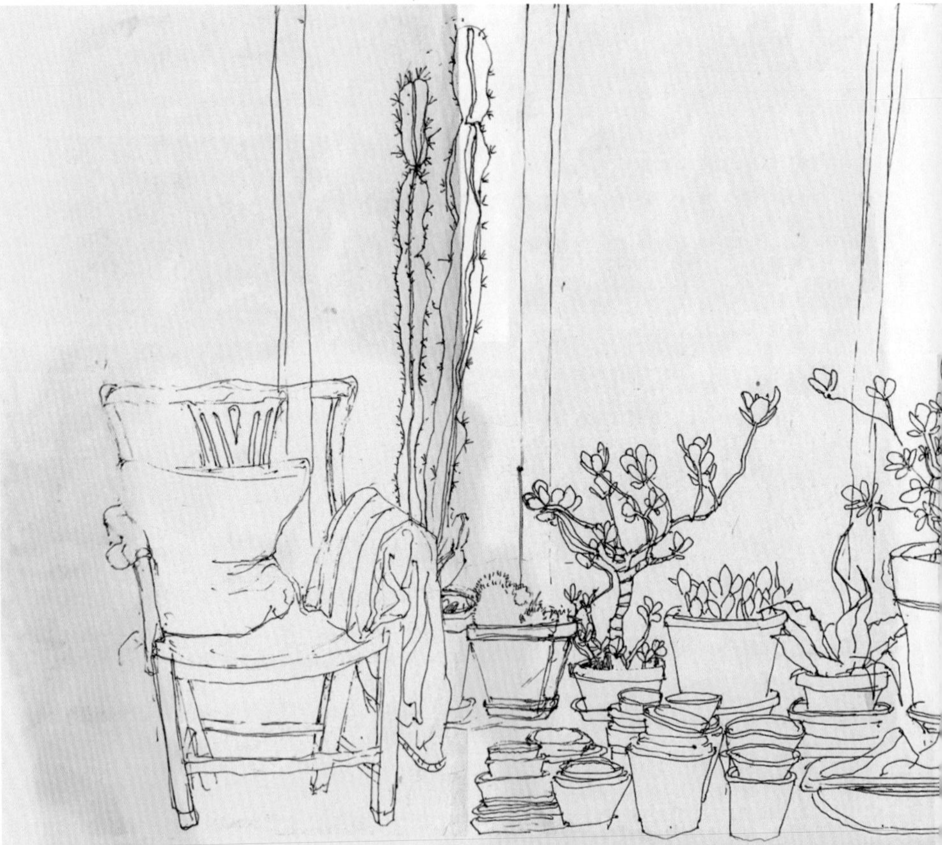

Jonny Bruce

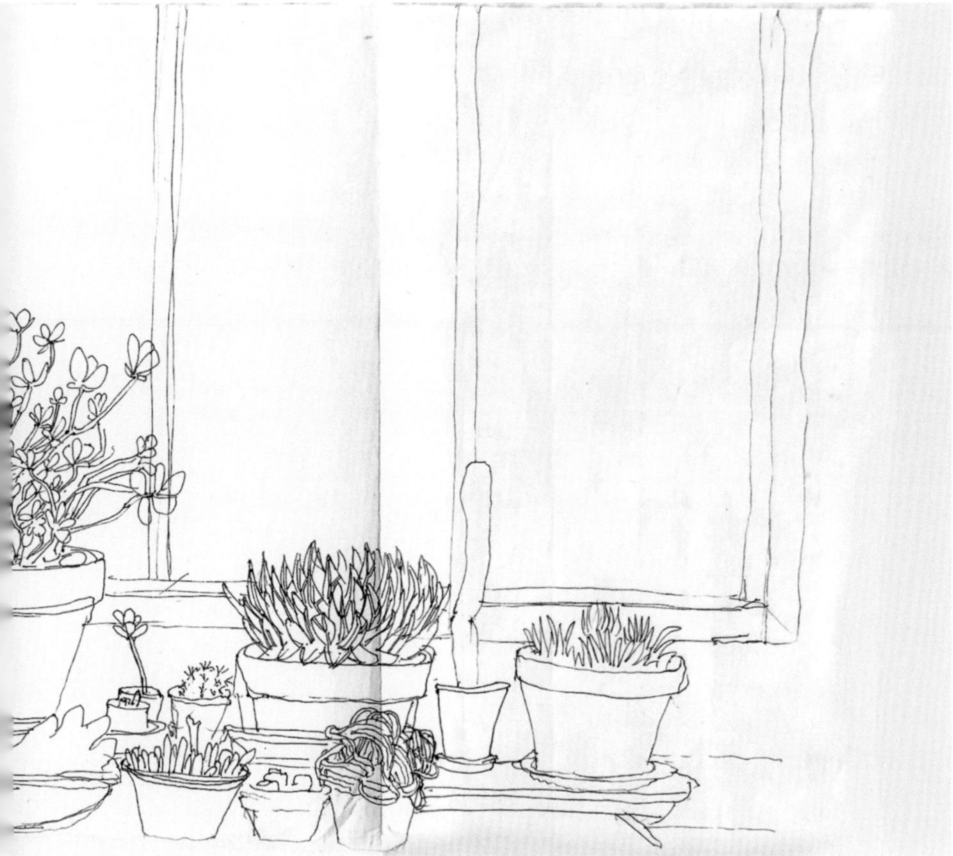

I remember how nervous I was to take on the responsibility for the garden and simply sitting and sketching helped both to calm me but also sharpen my focus.

Gardening New York City

In the early 1970s, Liz Christy, Amos Taylor and Martin Gallent founded the Green Guerillas. A band of guerrilla gardeners threw "seed green-aids" over the fences of vacant lots. They planted sunflower seeds in the center meridians of busy New York City streets. They put flower boxes on the window ledges of abandoned buildings.

Soon the Green Guerillas turned their attention to a large, debris-filled vacant lot on the corner of Bowery and Houston Streets. Where other people saw a vacant lot, they saw a community garden. They created the Bowery Houston Farm and Garden, and began rallying other people to use community gardening as a tool to reclaim urban land, stabilize city blocks, and get people working together to solve problems.

"It was a form of civil disobedience," recalls Amos Taylor. "We were basically saying to the government, if you won't do it, we will." The Green Guerillas weren't the only ones. They were part of a larger movement. All across the city, people were deciding to do something about the urban decay they saw all around them. Lower East Side residents Luis Torres and José Ayala started community gardening efforts in the early 1960s and 1970s, and environmentalist Hattie Carthan formed a youth greening corps to care for street trees in Bedford-Stuyvesant in 1971.

Soon, dozens of community gardens bloomed throughout New York City, and neighbors formed vital grassroots groups. Today, more than 600 community gardens serve as testaments to the skill, creativity, and determination of New York City's community gardeners.

Members of the W.124th Street Block Association Community
Garden clearing and showing love for the land.

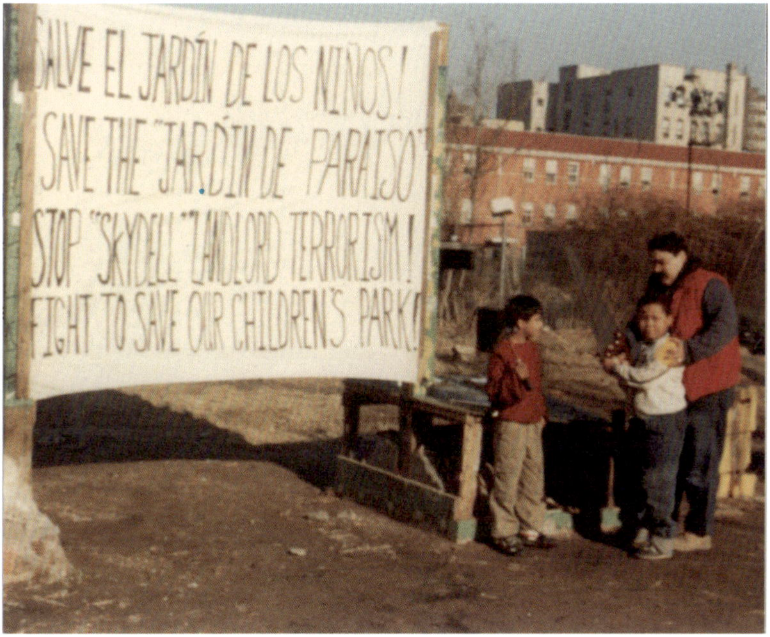
ALVE EL JARDÍN DE LOS NIÑOS!
SAVE THE "JARDÍN DE PARAISO"
STOP "SKYDELL" LANDLORD TERRORISM!
FIGHT TO SAVE OUR CHILDREN'S PARK!

Hundreds of community gardens in New York City came under threat in the 1990s when then-Mayor Rudolph Guiliani put them up for sale as 'vacant lots'. Green Guerillas worked as a strong advocate during city-wide protests and efforts to save the gardens.

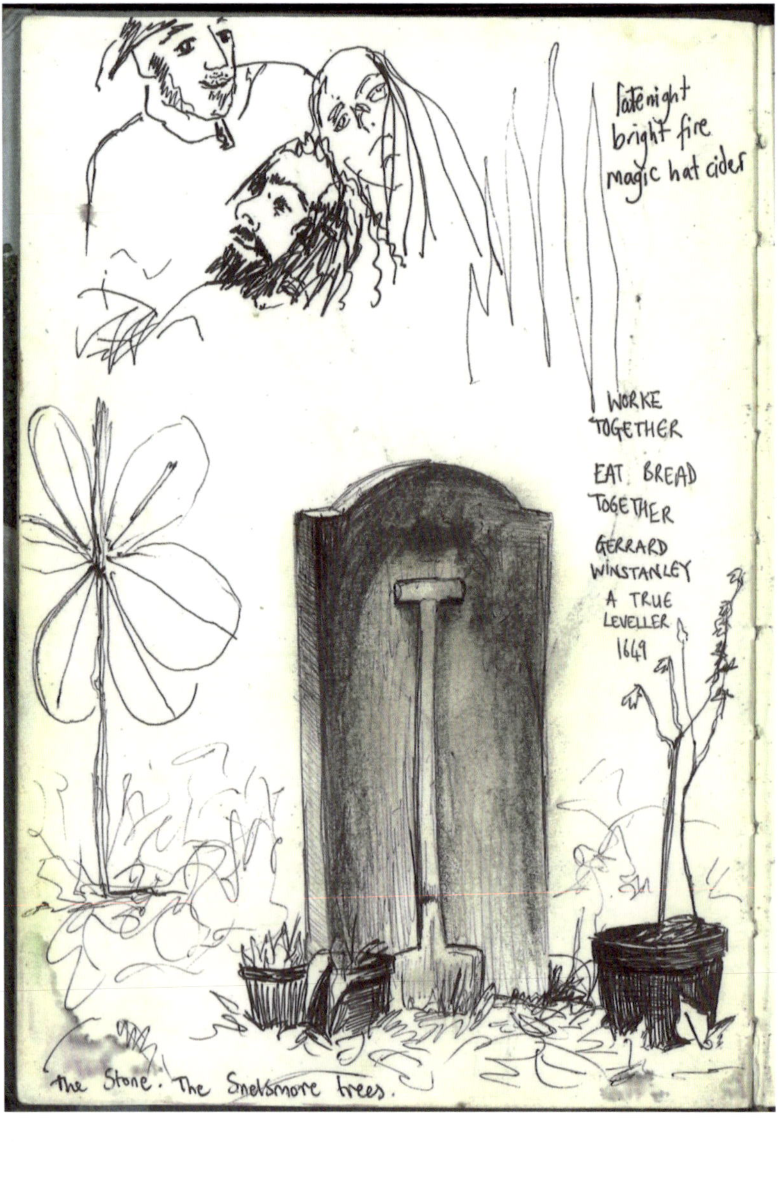
latenight
bright fire
magic hat cider
WORKE
TOGETHER
EAT BREAD
TOGETHER
GERRARD
WINSTANLEY
A TRUE
LEVELLER
1649
The Stone. The Snelsmore trees.

This is a drawing from St George's Hill, at a tree-planting & stone-laying ceremony in 1999 organised by The Land is Ours to celebrate the 350th anniversary of the Diggers occupation. The trees planted were seedlings that had been rescued from Snelsmore Common, at the Newbury Bypass protest.

Laura Joy

Gardening Interruptus

The first true activism of my life was for trees. I came back to New York
after the pandemic and heard that my local park East River Park which is
about a ten-minute bike ride from my apartment was going to be
demolished. I'd never heard of a park being destroyed and such a big juicy
one with a thousand trees many old, lots of drought resistant plants placed
there by the lower east side ecology center, a really cool non-profit that
picked up where the New York City Parks Dept. stopped which was pretty
much everywhere all over the city. New York spends less than 1% of its
budget on the Parks Dept. less than any other major American city. They
got away with this by privatizing parks. Big beautiful Central Park is
privately funded, has a conservancy that wealthy neighbors support.
Likewise Prospect Park in Brooklyn where all the dykes run their dogs has a
conservancy and their big fund-raising former Director is the now the head
of the Parks Department so you can imagine how much she cares about the
loss of big beautiful publicly funded parks in poor neighborhoods like mine.
I mean the East Village is largely flooded by NYU students these days and
baby carriages and bros of all sorts unlike its early junkie days when the
neighborhood was largely Puerto Rican and Ukrainian (they had kids too)
and then us, a shifting bunch of mainly white young people who came for
the drugs, low rent & art. But none of any of these people are the sort who
would start a conservancy to protect or save our park but the ecology center
which I mentioned for many years on no budget made it beautiful. And kids
volunteered, city kids who learned about growing things. It was a beautiful
vernacular growing monster. The best place. It was where you brought your
dog. The park also had a great running track, as well as an esplanade along

the river, lots of ball fields and a few tennis courts and a bandshell where dance parties and concerts happened. And there were barbecues all over the place for family holidays, largely Latinos. Kids grew up here, this was their yard, their park, their playground and that was their river and the trees dropped leaves and even fed the fish. It's half gone now and I spent a year and a half with a small gang of us which sometimes multiplied to a very large gang, 1500 people marched with us once to save the park but the problem was that people had been thinking for a while that Manhattan was an island and it was going to get flooded and what should we do and there were some really utopian plans but then a big storm happened, Sandy, a one in four hundred year storm and the park was flooded for literally two hours because essentially it was a gigantic sponge covered with trees that protected the neighborhood but in disaster capitalism this kind of moment is an opportunity. I mean New York has been going broke for years because cities really don't have ways of making money anymore once they stopped having industries there that paid taxes so they began in the seventies to sell the city to real estate, that's how New York City changed into the eighties and most politicians remained in office or got elected by making real estate deals and coastal resiliency was hot when big crook Bill DeBlasio came into office (Mayor) and he pretty much sold our park to a real estate consultancy called HR & A and we could protest our asses off but the newspapers in New York also survive on real estate. They made it be that they were saving this poor neighborhood, by destroying their park and building a new one on top of it. The New York Times doesn't even have a metro section anymore so when we pitched op eds about the tragedy of destroying one of New York's great parks, half of New York City's pair of lungs, the editorial board said nope, too *local*. New York is not an anywhere now, it's an idea.

I came here to Texas to sulk after that (I'm privileged though not luxuriously so) and write too and someplace in my torpor while walking my dog in town I noticed all the trees were dying. There's been a drought people explained. I guess I did notice it never rained. Last summer I noticed that *my* trees were dying. I have two big pinyons in front of my house. The guy who sold the place to me once came by with his wife when I sadly was not in town and what he wanted was to see how those two trees he and his father had planted were doing. I'm glad he came *that* year. I got all the tree guys and the water guys to come around and they explained something I never knew which was that you need to water trees. I mean really? Once they were established I thought they were just there. So I bought hoses and sprinklers and alfalfa and just made a beautiful warm collar of care around their roots and flooded those fucking trees one night a week and now they are okay. My trees are going to make it. I mean how could I be fighting for trees that are getting cut down in New York and not notice that the two tall trees in front of my house that make it shady are dying. But they're not. So I handled it well.

I am a plant killer in general. There's that daily care plants want, the water and the conversation I don't get. A dog barks, you take it for a walk. And I began to walk around my town and notice how badly still all the trees are doing. But there are glorious ones too. I don't know the names of trees and I suspect I never will. Big windy thick thorough trees. There are apps but my photographs tend to just sit there unknown. Then this thing came over me and this is really all I've got to say. I know a guy in my town named Jim Martinez and he takes people on walks in this high desert museum of local plants and trees and Jim tells you what everything is and I forget immediately but I take pictures and I love strolling through the green, the brown and the white and the pink all the colors of growing things. It's soft. I like hiking. I like walking in the woods. I said Jim I wonder if you can tell me how I can get more trees. Once I saved those two I thought maybe I could have more. I have like a third of an acre of cactus and tumbleweed and brown grasses around my house. I never cared. I mean I didn't know. I thought it was nice. He said yeah I can get you some trees. What do you want. Oh god what do I want. That changed my routine. I was walking through my town looking at the trees that were beautiful and were doing really well. Not dying, not dead. The opportunity to get trees changed my focus. I took pictures and sent them to him. Maybe some grasses too. Grasses are good he said. He's a calm man. I didn't do the labor. I have no interest. I water, that's what I do. One day I went for a workshop at the Chinati foundation to plant trees and I planted one with Morgan Bassichis, the great singer and comedian and anti-zionist Jew. He did most of the digging I admit. I don't really want to dig. So all the stuff is now in my yard, Jim did it with help. From Gabriella and Juan, who work for him. He gave me a recipe – the grasses get watered for ten minutes, a trickle, every two days. The trees get a half hour every third day. And then I have a day off. So here's the thing, the way you water plants is you sit down at your desk and you begin to work – on something important. You write or edit. You can read but it's really fun to do something deep and engaging. You set your phone to ten minutes. And the bell rings. I currently like one called "summit" which is a lot of triumphal horns and birds. At first you think are those real birds. It's an inspiring alarm. And you go move the hose. Like I have twenty-four clumps of grasses and I have three hoses. That means in a stretch of work and watering I stop eight times and get up and move the hoses. I think I am so distracted a person that I feel kind of moored or the act of watering kind of firms up or syncopates my writing practice.

When I do the trees I can do yoga or meditate. Trees is more of a bodily watering day. After that I get to write but I'm really steady now having taking care of my friends and having stretched and been still. The trees have names. Gregg is the less healthy live oak. Hannah is the thriving one. Barbara is the Cypress and the red bud has no name but it's coming. Perhaps Lucy. There's no end to this story because tomorrow is trees. Meanwhile the aloe plants in my house are dying. I need to repot them. That's dirt. I don't do dirt. People keep giving me aloe plants. I don't know why. Don't.

Just to be completely anti-memorial, it *never* strikes me that the trees that I've planted have anything to do with East River Park or mourning. Maybe saving the two big old ones did that.

What I think is going on is that I am growing something that will keep growing when *I* die. I think it's bold to plant trees in a war racked planet, in a dying empire, when I could see them grow for twenty years and then someone else will watch them. I did that. Death is the biggest interruptus of all and I'm for it. It's wild and free and several of my trees, I hope, will be enormous.

Eileen Myles

Rosemary Mayer

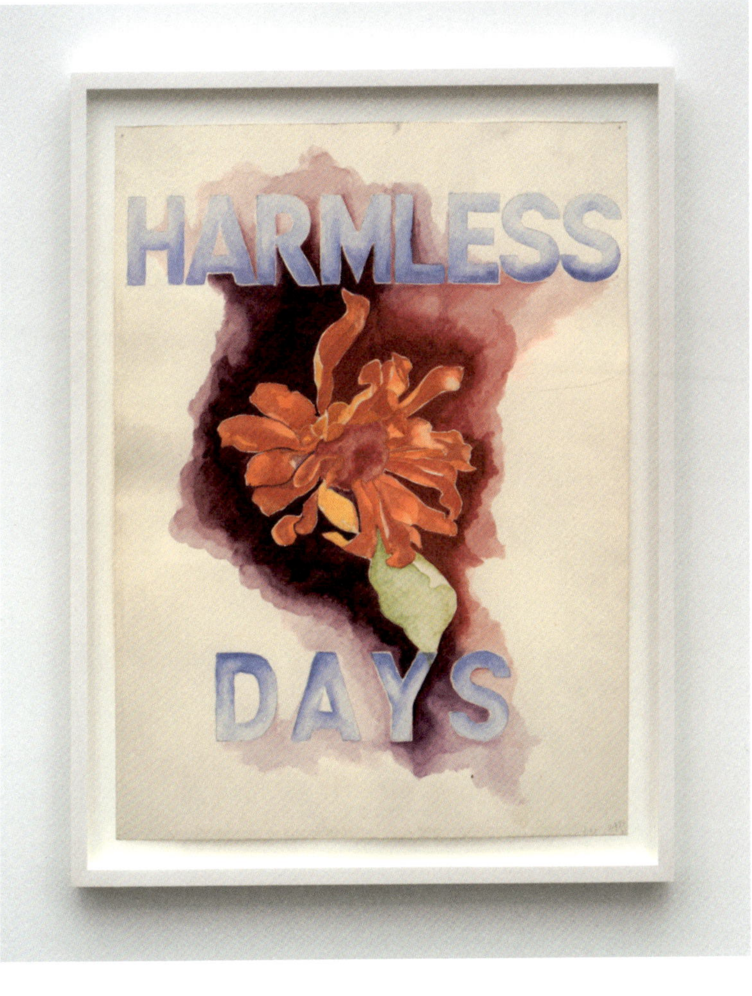
HARMLESS
DAYS

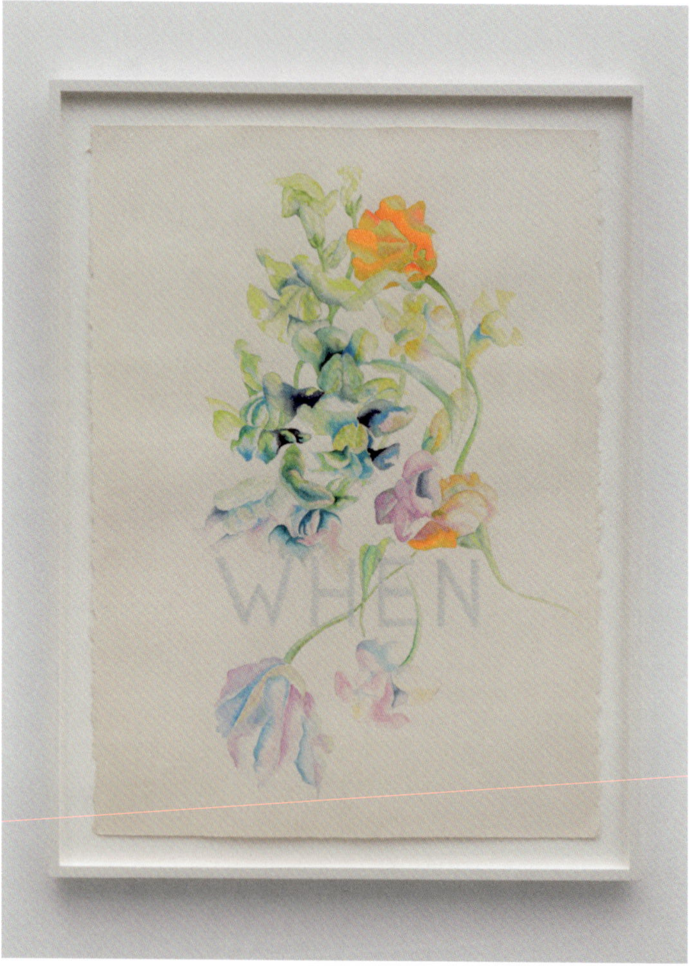
WHEN

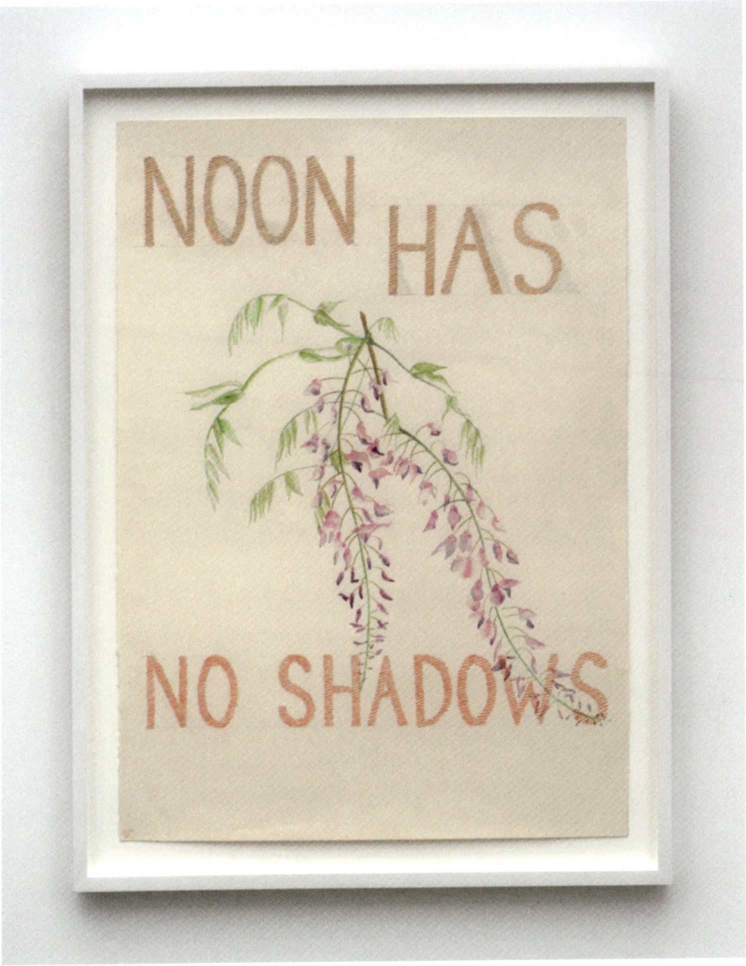
NOON HAS
NO SHADOWS

1. *HARMLESS DAYS*, 1983
Watercolour and graphite on paper

2. *WHEN*, 1983
Watercolor, colored pencil, and graphite on paper

3. *NOON HAS NO SHADOWS*, 1983
Watercolor, colored pencil, and graphite on paper

Courtesy of the Estate of Rosemary Mayer

The Garden

for Adam Purple

Close to a house on a piece of ground
For the growing of vegetables, flowers & fruits
On fertile well-developed land
Is a delightful place or state, a paradise
Often a place for public enjoyment
Where grows the alyssum to cure our rage

Oriental night of the careless developers
Carpet of snow of the drugged landlords
Basket of gold the city's confused
Royal carpet of its bureaucracies,
Bored with bombs
Political ones of the complicated governments
blow stick up the very orb
For its nonmetal yet golden remains

Competing with the larval corn borers
The salaried test-borers
Imminently lead anti-sexually down to the foundation
Of the annihilation
Of a circular garden in which live members of
the mustard family
The tomato or nightshade family
The poppy family
The geranium family
The aster family
The mint family
The thistle or aster family
The violet family (heartsease)
The lily family
The cucumber or gourd family
The rose family
The composite or daily family
The parsley or carrot family

And other families
(I don't think the pokeweed family lives there,
It earns too little or too much money per year)

We are told to swallow not a rainbow
But like the celandine the juicy proposal
That the lemon balm of low income housing,
Applied like agerartum to the old Lower East Side
(As early matured as the apricot)
And probably turned by deeply divided leaves
Like a rape of grapes before it's all over
Cannot coexist with the gleaming black raspberries
Is an ancient abandoned place
Around Eldridge, Foresight and Stanton Streets

We're asked not to think, like pansies do
That the pinnately compound, ovate, lanceloate, non-linear,
        lobed, compound, toothed, alternate, opposite,
        palmate, heart-shaped, stalkless, clasping,
        perfoliate, and basal rosette-ish leaves
Can heal like the comfrey
And cause to grow together
The rough hairy leaves of the city's people and
        the rough hairy leaves of the sublimity of
        a gardener's art
Made with vegetarian shit and free as cupid's darts

If all our eyes had the clarity of apples
In a world as altered
As if by the wood betony
And all kinds of basil were the only riders of the land
It would be good to be together
Both under and above the ground
To be sane as the madwort,
Ripe as corn, safe as sage,
Various as dusty miller and hens & chickens,
In politics as kindly fierce and dragonlike as tarragon,
Revolutionary as the lily.

Bernadette Mayer
'The Garden' was originally published in
A Bernadette Mayer Reader, New Directions, 1992

Courtesy of the Estate of Bernadette Mayer

Unknown artist
Detail of a painted wall from a room in The House of the Orchard,
Pompeii, c. 150 BCE, excavated 1951-52

Savaged Gardens

The first thing my grandmother did after the death of my mother, her only daughter, was to tend to the single, purple جهنمية tree—the only harbinger of colour amid the austerity of the marble cenotaphs—that she had planted few decades prior. So ubiquitous is the جهنمية (bougainvillea) in the Mediterranean region that it is hard to imagine a time when it didn't inject its urgent colour into the desert-drab landscape. But like so much else— tomatoes, eucalyptus—we think of as indigenous to the ancient lands of the Great Sea, the bougainvillea was a New World intruder. It's said the flowering tree was brought to Cairo from the Spanish Americas by the Egyptian battalion of soldiers sent to Vera Cruz in 1863 to prop up the rule of the first and last European emperor of Mexico Maximilian I, executed by firing squad only four years later.

While Egyptians took to the tree's brilliant colours, they never took to a name borrowed from the title of the French explorer Louis-Antoine, Comte de Bougainville. Instead they called it جهنمية, the infernal one. Derived from the Quranic word for hell, the plant is said to only glow in sweltering places like an unshaded cemetery. The word جنينة for garden, was a diminutive of جنة for Paradise. That this hellish flower would provide the only ember of colour in a place otherwise surrounded by invocations and evocations of a beige heaven, always seemed appropriate to me. My grandmother looked after the lone bougainvillea over her daughter's grave until she herself was buried under it four years ago.

It isn't a coincidence that we metaphorically, euphemistically describe the displacement of peoples from their homes as 'uprooting'. The massacre of a thousand protestors in Rabi'a square in Cairo that announced President Sisi's coup in 2013 was accompanied by a decade-long assault on the historic trees of Cairo and the gardens that housed them. The verdant agricultural belt around the city—containing some of the Nile Valley's most fertile fields—has been eradicated, nearly entirely. Where there were once fields of cotton, now stand unfinished red-brick and concrete towers piercing the sky line. Entire villages of people living in once-green pastures have been expelled from their ancestral homes. Within Cairo itself, the military junta's bulldozers now surround the walled gardens that grow amid the mausolea of the nearly two-millennia old City of the Dead where my mother joined ancestors buried in the cemetery since the eighteenth century and where over a million of the country's poorest are said to live. Like planets in an orbit, the tombs surround the sanctuaries of holy women and saints.

The bulldozers came a few months after my grandmother was laid to rest. Red arrows were spray-painted on the exterior walls of thousands of mausolea, along with a single ominous term: عزل, an injunction that means displace, excommunicate, isolate, depose, sequester, cut off. Several weeks later, the junta announced its plans for the wholescale demolition of the entire City of the Dead, part of a UNESCO World Heritage protected site, to build a highway cruelly named "The Passageway to Paradise." Hearing that the bulldozers were circling his dead ancestors like vultures to carrion, a friend rushed to the gravesite of his grandfather, one of the country's most significant mid-century novelists, only to find the site desecrated. Where there had been a serene walled garden in the courtyard were now unidentified shards of bone strewn amid the rusty tin cans of ghee that had been repurposed into planters before the sanctuary had been violated.

When my mother died at age fourteen and was buried there, I consoled myself with the knowledge that she lay in a place of staggering beauty and that one day I too would be laid to rest beside her. But with the announcement of the military junta's vision to displace thousands of dead corpses and the one million plus people—undertakers, caretakers, florists, calligraphers, professional mourners—that live around them, I felt a sharp severing of the umbilical chord that attached me in my mind to my mother and motherland alike.

Since the sentence was pronounced, now four years ago, it has yet to be executed. Like the disappearance of dissidents to locations unknown and the trial of revolutionaries for crimes undisclosed, we the grieving are held in bureaucratic suspense, a form of collective torture that renders us into pliant, pliable, political supplicants at the hands of a vengeful tyrant that won't be appeased. I often dream of what I'll do with my mother's bones, the bones of the eight generations of ancestors that surround her and the marmoreal monuments that, for better or for worse, have pressed us into this cruel land.

Amid brewing rage at the decision to destroy the medieval city's spiritual centre, the junta wants to relocate and reconstruct the most historically significant of these sites in an open air museum. But only perversion allows for a calculus that makes a hierarchy out of human life on, above all, aesthetic grounds. History's logic is as violent and arbitrary as the generals that unleash it. If the junta has its way, our remains will become relics like the mummies of our ancient predecessors. Displayed in temperature-controlled vitrines of too-brightly lit museums, we will become monuments to a despot's hubris, testament to the pleasures that the generals take in our pain.

*

Since October 7th 2023, across the border, zionist militias have accelerated their assault on the gnarly-barked olive trees, several thousand years old, that rooted the Palestinians to their ancient homeland. Just as in Egypt, such arboreal sadism accompanies exhumations of bodies, some freshly-buried and some already disintegrated. Through their assault on the ancestors in the earth and the historic trees that guard them, the regimes either side of the Sinai Peninsula reinscribe the unwritten covenant that binds a people to their land with genocidal new histories, disguised as old. By prising open the past, of Pharaohs or Pharisees, the warlords augur the coming of a terrifying future.

The gardens—Cairo's last lung, the one place where birdsong could still be heard—are to be poured over in concrete just as pine trees were planted in the Holy Land to cover over the crimes of Ben Gurion's henchmen and to make of Palestine a Switzerland. Turning the desert green is a threat—to bury the evidence—not a promise of rebirth. It is no coincidence that the word culture (as in horticulture, agriculture) used to refer to tilling, to honouring the land until the beginning of the nineteenth century. It perversely makes sense therefore the genocidal assault on a people and their collective forms of remembering is so often accompanied by an uprooting of their trees, their gardens and their orchards.

*

I want to be free from History. I want to be buried in a garden of mandrakes.

It is said that of all the plants, only a mandrake—a sweet-scented, stemless shrub native to Egypt and Palestine—can protest its own uprooting. Like a steadfast warrior defending the dead, the plant will shriek should the generals and their thugs come for its roots. Those who hear its scream when it is uprooted will be struck dead.

When flowering, the mandrake—*mandragora officinarum*, brain-thief, master of life-breath, love's apple, devil's testicle—produces the natural world's highest concentration of a substance called atropine in its roots. Named after Atropos, the Fate that chooses how we die, atropine causes constipation, the drying of dying people's mouths (a cure for death rattle), and to dilate pupils as wide as those of a man in extreme arousal or on the verge of death.

I want to be buried with the seditious flower of the disobedient.

It was said that Avicenna in the 11th century believed that the mandrake plant grew out of the splattered semen of executed men, hanging dead from the gallows. The philosopher also reported that a king named Absal who could not bring himself to lie with a woman was advised by a sage to impregnate a mandrake root instead. Further west, across Europe, witches were rumored to gather below mandrakes to impregnate themselves with the plant's root.

It was on grounds of possession of a mandrake root that Joan of Arc was found guilty. Her person was an embodiment of the increasingly inescapable overlap between sexual deviancy, religious heresy and political dissidence. The word "faggot", after all, comes from the Latin *fagus,* or "beech tree." From the Greek *phagus,* which means any tree bearing edible nut or fruit. In classical Greek, *phagos* especially referred to oak trees. The old fairy tree near Domremy where Joan of Arc first heard her voices was a *fagus* tree. Heretics were burned on bundles of faggots. Her killing at the stake was a foretelling.

It is fitting therefore that the mandrake would become a symbol of the excess people—queers and heretics—themselves an embodiment of what must be excised for abstractions like the nation-state to thrive. From the perspective of such states, the uprooting of undesirable peoples and their obstructive memories is a process of weeding, of removing those that stand in the way of a vision of historical progress "flourishing", a word that has clear horticultural "roots". Israeli officials notoriously refer to the country's periodic bombardments of Gaza as "mowing the lawn."

I want a salve for my pain, for the pain of the dead.

Squeezed into a juice and mixed with opium, hemlock, henbane, ivy, mulberry, hops, and wild lettuce, the mandrake forms the basis of *Spongia somnifera*: the world's first anaesthetic. Modern-day anaesthetics, the mandrake's descendants, are prohibited in Gaza today, along with fabric for clothing, A4 paper, pasta, biscuits, musical instruments, cardamom, coriander, cumin, ginger, nutmeg and sage, jam, chicks, notebooks, sewing machines, cement, toys, donkeys, pens, and pencils. In Gaza today, a prophecy of our future, scalpel blades have to be reused in surgeries, but with time they have become too blunt to do what they are supposed to do. In January 2024, Hani Bseiso amputated his 17-year-old niece's leg with a kitchen knife from his home, using only his clothes to stop the bleeding and dish soap as antiseptic. When interviewed, Bseiso's niece, Ahed said, "There was no anaesthesia. My anaesthesia was the Quran which I was reciting".

*

Analgesic; anaesthetic; alibi; arcane allegory; Hand-of-Glory; elf-rune; the *mens rea* of a transvestite saint; "Viagra of the valleys"; a cure for barrenness as old as the Bible, with two roots that look like human legs. Sweet-scented, soporific, seminal, seditious flower of criminal cum. O Mandrake—you resist your own uprooting and in so doing contain the secret that will allow us to forget.

"History will judge them"—a lie, repeated not believed, a consolation of the impotent to the stupid. There will be no Greek chorus. No voiceover like in the movies.

And in any case, I neither want feigned memory nor forced forgetting. I want to be free of History. I want to punish them for stealing my sleep. I don't want to be buried under a bougainvillea, but a mandrake. Howling and numb, forgotten but never forgiving, I write to take revenge on a meaning that doesn't yet exist.

Hussein Omar

Joy Gregory
Manchineel Tree, Little Apples of Death (1), 2021
From the Plants of Resistance series

Courtesy of the artist

Manchineel Tree
Little Apples of Death

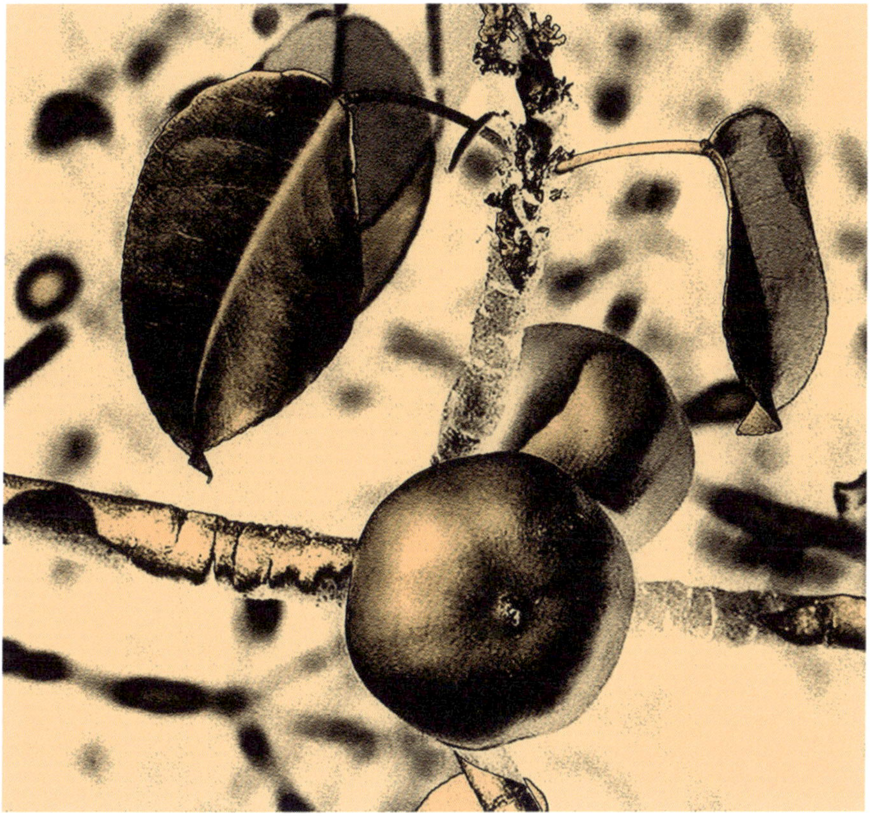

The indigenous people of the Caribbean
used the sap of the manchineel to poison their arrows and
the toxic leaves to contaminate the water supply of the invading Spaniards

from 'Remembrances', 1832

By Langley Bush I roam, but the bush hath left its hill,
On Cowper Green I stray, tis a desert strange and chill,
And spreading Lea Close oak, ere decay had penned its will
To the axe of the spoiler and self-interest fell a prey
And Crossberry Way and old Round Oak's narrow lane
With its hollow trees like pulpits I shall never see again.
Enclosure like a Buonaparte let not a thing remain,
It levelled every bush and tree and levelled every hill
And hung the moles for traitors - though the brook is running still
It runs a naked brook, cold and chill

Northborough Jany 13 1836

My dear Henderson,

Will you have the kindness to give me a few shrubs & flowers
a few woodbines and something my wife likes she calls
everlasting have you got a drooping willow & double
blossomed furze   my wife also wants a red japonica
      I am hardly able to say more

God bless you | yours ever

John Clare

John Clare

Alison Lloyd
Houseplant, **1977**
35mm film photograph

Courtesy of the Estate of Alison Lloyd

Alison Lloyd
Ogden Brook collaboration with Glassball Studio on the Peak District National Park Boundary, 25 August 2022

Courtesy of the Estate of Alison Lloyd

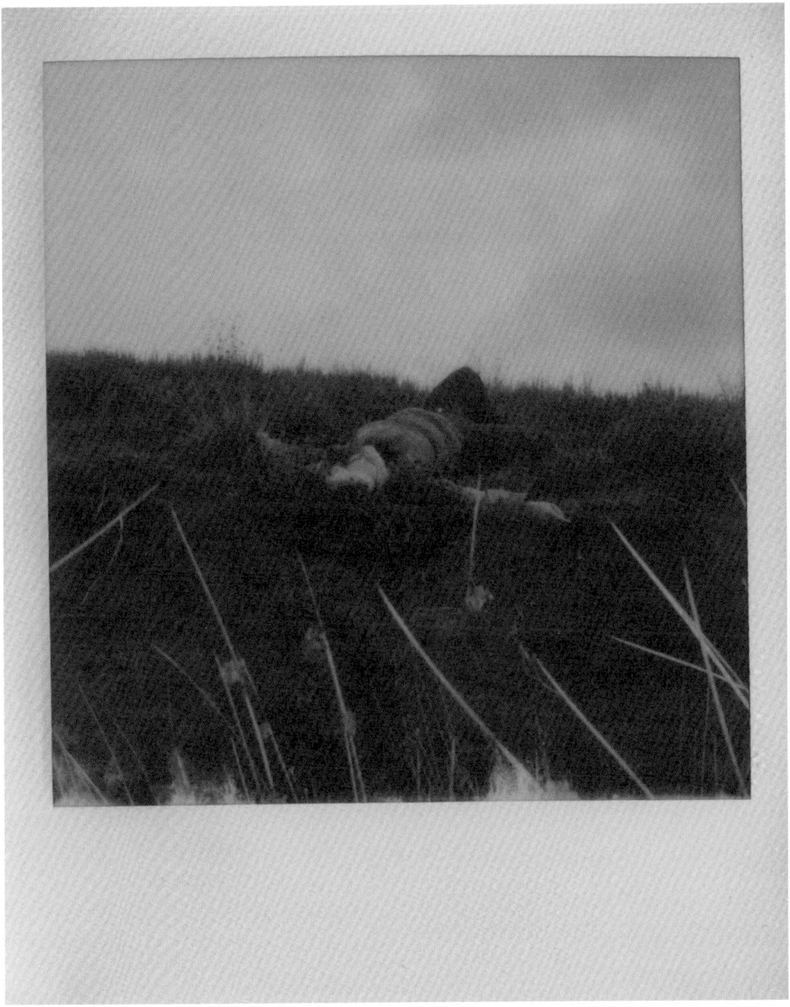

Hilary Lloyd
Orpheus looks back in the Underworld
"Oh my god I'm gorgeous"

Courtesy of the artist

On Little Sparta

In the spring of 1995, I traveled by train from Brighton to Edinburgh to visit Little Sparta, the garden of the poet Ian Hamilton Finlay. A friend in Vancouver had given me Finlay's phone number, and during my month in England—my first book had just been published, and it was my first trip overseas to participate in poetry readings and festivals—I, with great nervousness, phoned him in order to organize a date for my visit. He was recalcitrant at first, requesting several times that I call again the following week to check whether the new grass had germinated. He did not want a too-early spring visitor to see the temple to Apollo before the grass was up. Finally he agreed to my visit—it helped that he had a soft spot for Canadian poets, as opposed to a mysterious tribe he referred to as "the curators"— and I travelled north by train to meet the poet-gardener who had inspired my own recent researches in pastoral poetics.

After a night in a cheap B&B, kippers for breakfast, a visit to MacDiarmid's tomb, and a climb up the uneven steps to Robbie Burns' house, I took the agreed-upon bus. His gardener met me in a hatchback at a bus stop at the edge of a field near nothing else. I had expected to recognize the garden's follies glittering near the horizon, but I saw only sheep. He had a gardener because he did not particularly like attending to the demands of plants. Almost every part of his work was collaborative, I knew that, so why shouldn't the growing be also? I was incoherent with excitement arriving at the gravel car park, being met by Mr. Finlay, and being served by him a cup of strong tea in his screened-in porch. We sat and talked and he asked for news of Stephen Scobie, bpNichol and Doug Barbour, the Canadian poets he knew, and of Coach House Books, which had published some of his early work in the 70s. He told me about the latest battles in his war with the Scottish Arts Council. I gave him my new book. Then he disappeared indoors, and I began my slow investigation of the place. The garden seemed small, much smaller than photographs had led me to anticipate, yet it was extremely dense. I took many notes, and many photographs. Later I discovered that in my excited clumsiness I had loaded the film in my new camera incorrectly, and all of my photos were moot. This was a Petri micro, a defunct Japanese compact automatic, which I had just bought in an Edinburgh camerashop especially to be able to take slide images of the garden, my intention then being to later make a slide lecture. I still have the camera and have not used it since.

Little Sparta was organized on the nineteenth century landscape principle of garden rooms, each of a slightly different scale, and each serving as a kind of laboratory or workshop for the elaboration of a specific group of concepts and propositions. There was the part that brought together the pre-Socratic philosophers with a typology of aircraft carriers executed as stone garden benches. There was a Rousseauian part of labeled trees that intersected with the French Revolutionary part. A row of windowsill clay flowerpots was labeled with the names of women of the French Revolution. I diligently wrote down their names, and later Mr. Finlay told me that this work referred to a series by Anselm Kiefer. There was a part that cited German Romantic poets, where a Hölderlinian rose overhung a pool, and it was here that Mr. Finlay emerged from his cottage at five-ish, dressed only in a large white bath sheet, toga-style, and asking whether I minded if he took his bath. I quite expected him to drop the toga and dive buff into

Image of Little Sparta courtesy Wikipedia

Apollo's pool, but he disappeared again into his house. I was taking longer
than he had expected, and this was because this garden, although not vast,
was an intensely figured tissue of installation, citation and reference, and I
wanted to cherish and annotate each text, name and image that I was able
to recognize. Time thickened up in the garden: germination time and tea-
time and bath-time.

Out behind the house and temple the scale was widest, and there, Daphne,
in cut-out stainless steel painted green, fled to a grove, and there was the
cave where Aeneas and Dido sheltered from the storm, amorously slowing
the founding of Rome. I noted everything, and when I had finished I was
offered a second cup of tea on the porch. I asked questions, jotted down
phrases and names, expressed my gratitude and was driven back by the
gardener to catch the Edinburgh bus. The next morning I visited the

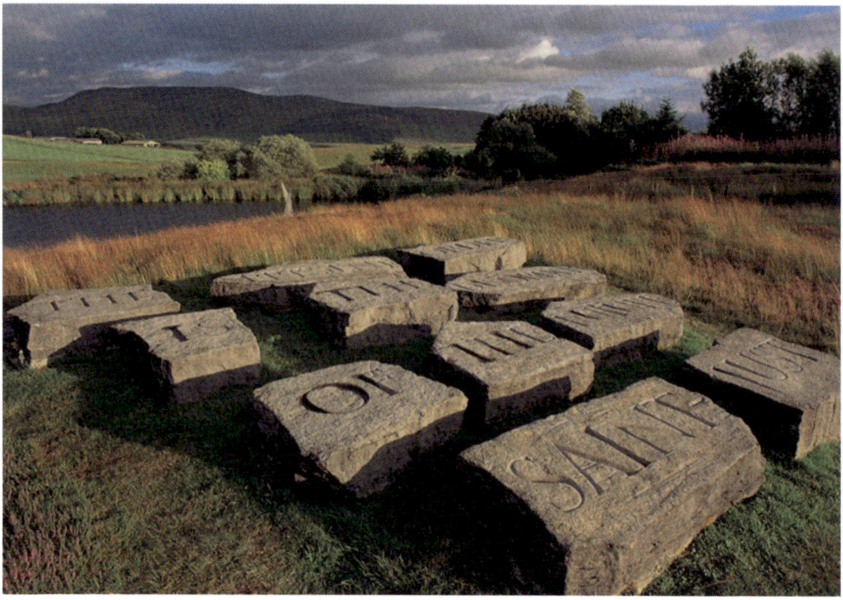
OF

Image of Little Sparta courtesy Wikipedia

bookshop of the Scottish National Gallery of Modern Art, where I had learned I could buy ephemeral publications from Finlay's Wild Hawthorn Press. Looking through files and choosing some postcards and leaflets, I realized how the garden served as an experimental hub from which these dispatches and others could be issued; whether in stone or on paper the concrete poems referred back to the inventive working site of Little Sparta. Years later in my travels, coming across Finlay installations in the garden at the Serpentine Gallery in London, the garden at the Fondation Cartier in Paris, on the campus at University of California San Diego, or in catalogues dug up in used bookshops, this notion was strengthened. Without moving from Little Sparta, Finlay directed the distant installation of concepts that had as their single Epicurean origin his thinking garden.

Back home in Vancouver it was now obvious that, first of all, I had to read all of Rousseau. I did so. That became most of the rest of my work since then.

Lisa Robertson

g1 generation one

g2 generation two

g3 (g1 × g2, g2 × g2)

g4 (g1 × g2, g2 × g2, g2 × g3, g3 × g3)

g5 (g1 × g2, g2 × g2, g2 × g3, g3 × g3, g1 × g4,
g2 × g4, g3 × g4, g4 × g4)

g6 (g1 × g2, g2 × g2, g2 × g3, g3 × g3, g1 × g4
g2 × g5, g3 × g5, g4 × g5, g5 × g5, g1 × g5)

g7 (g1 × g2, g2 × g2, g2 × g3, g3 × g3, g1 × g4
g2 × g5, g3 × g5, g4 × g5, g2 × g6, g3 × g6, g4
g6, g5 × g6, g6 × g6, g1 × g7, g2 × g7, g3 × g7
g4 × g7, g5 × g7, g6 × g7, g7 × g7)

g8 (g1 × g2, g2 × g2, g2 × g3, g3 × g3, g1 × g4
g2 × g4, g3 × g4, g4 × g4, g4 × g5, g4 × g6
g4 × g7, g4 × g8, g5 × g5, g5 × g6, g5 × g7,
g5 × g8, g6 × g7, g6 × g8, g6 × g1, g7 × g7,
g7 × g2, g3 × g7, g4 × g7, g5 × g7, g6 × g
g7 × g8, g8 × g8)

g9 (g1 × g2, g2 × g2, g2 × g3, g3 × g3, g1 × g4
g2 × g5, g2 × g6, g2 × g7, g2 × g8, g3 × g4, g3 × g
g3 × g5, g3 × g6, g3 × g7, g3 × g8, g3 × g9, g4 × g4
g4 × g5, g4 × g6, 4 × g7, g5 × g8, g5 × g9, g6 × g7,

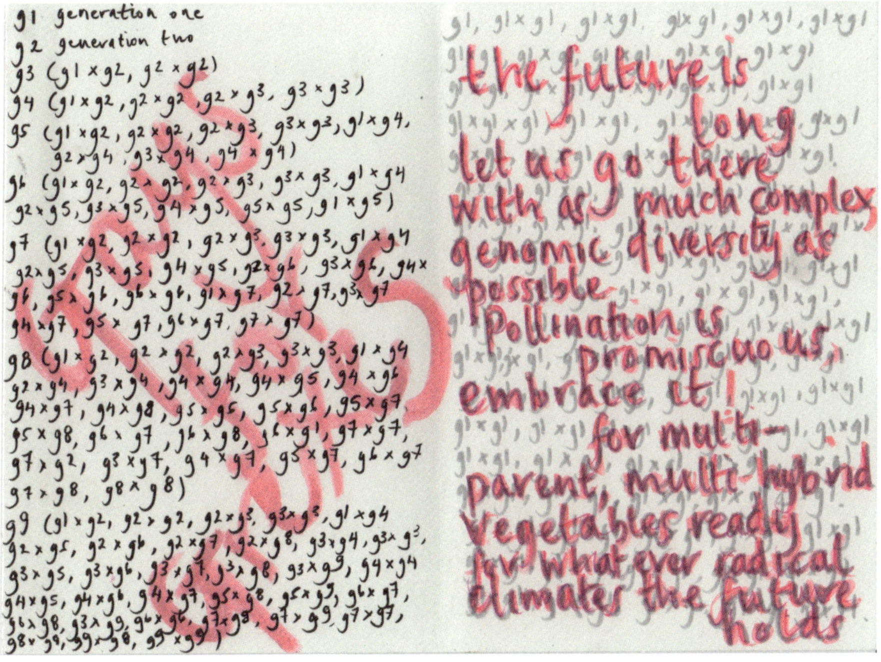

g1 generation one
g2 generation two
g3 (g1 × g2, g2 × g2)
g4 (g1 × g2, g2 × g2, g2 × g3, g3 × g3)
g5 (g1 × g2, g2 × g2, g2 × g3, g3 × g3, g1 × g4, g2 × g4, g3 × g4, g4 × g4)
g6 (g1 × g2, g2 × g2, g2 × g3, g3 × g3, g1 × g4
g2 × g5, g3 × g5, g4 × g5, g5 × g5, g1 × g5)
g7 (g1 × g2, g2 × g2, g2 × g3, g3 × g3, g1 × g4
g2 × g5, g3 × g5, g4 × g5, g2 × g6, g3 × g6, g4 ×
g4 × g7, g5 × g7, g6 × g7, g7 × g7)
g8 (g1 × g2, g2 × g2, g2 × g3, g3 × g3, g1 × g4
g2 × g4, g3 × g4, g4 × g4, g4 × g5, g4 × g6
g4 × g7, g4 × g8, g5 × g5, g5 × g6, g5 × g7
g5 × g8, g6 × g7, g6 × g8, g6 × g1, g7 × g7,
g7 × g2, g3 × g7, g4 × g7, g5 × g7, g6 × g7
g7 × g8, g8 × g8)
g9 (g1 × g2, g2 × g2, g2 × g3, g3 × g3, g1 × g4
g2 × g6, g2 × g6, g2 × g7, g2 × g8, g3 × g4, g3 × g3,
g3 × g5, g3 × g6, g3 × g7, g3 × g8, g3 × g9, g4 × g4
g4 × g5, g4 × g6, g4 × g7, g5 × g8, g6 × g7,
g6 × g8, g3 × g9, g4 × g9, g7 × g9, g7 × g9,
g8 × g9, g9 × g9, g9 × g9)

the future is
long
let us go there
with as much complex
genomic diversity as
possible
Pollination is
promiscuous,
embrace it!
for multi-
parent, multi-hybrid
vegetables ready
for whatever radical
climates the future
holds

Alys Fowler
<——— *this is what we could do; this is what we do.*

175

Sarah Wood

Actions to imagine:

The Garden of the Internationale

Sarah Wood

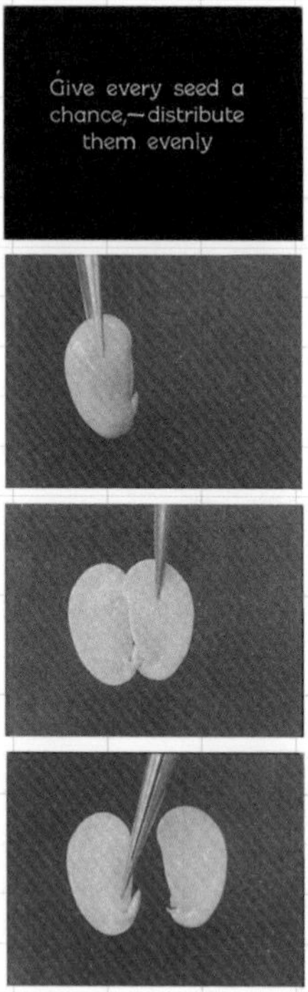
Give every seed a
chance,—distribute
them evenly

1. Welcome the wandering plants
   of the planet

Go and sit in a garden.

Spend some time taking in everything
that surrounds you.

Notice which plant in particular
catches your eye.

Find out the name of the plant.

Find out where that plant originates.

Honour that plant by tracing the
journey made by its ancestors.

One day make that journey yourself.

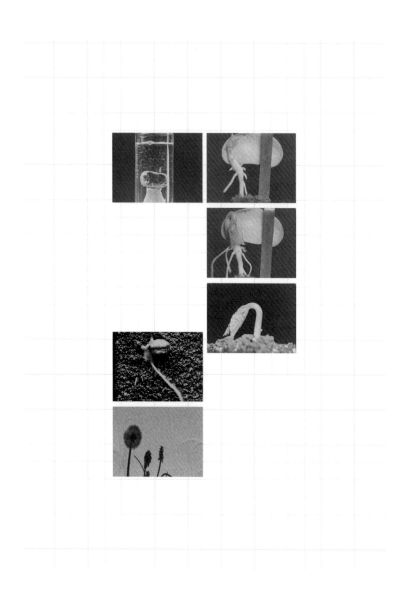

2. Take a map for a walk round the
   garden

Mark an 'X' on a blank sheet of
paper.

Mark a second 'X' on another part
of the same page.

Draw a route between the two X's like
you're drawing a treasure map.

Pick up the piece of paper and take
it outside into a garden, any garden.

Follow the map route you've made in
your drawing to navigate the garden.

Spend some time understanding the
place where it leads you.

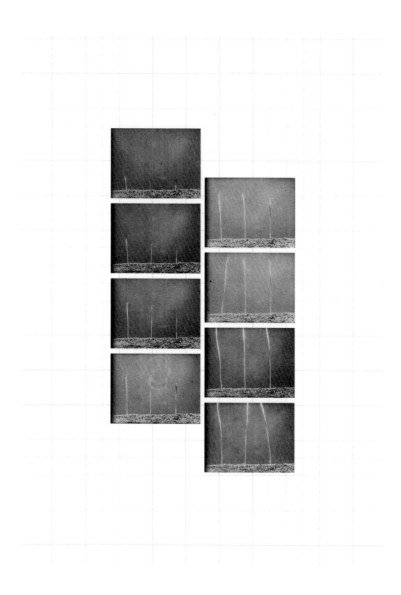

3. Hurry up slow down!

Find an open space in a garden.

Walk as fast as you can backwards
and forwards across the space over
and over again.

Hurry up!

Keep crossing the space until you
feel that you've raised your body
temperature a little.

As soon as you do lie down exactly
where you are.

As you lie still notice how long
it takes for your body to cool down.

As you lie still enjoy how long it
takes to tune into the world around
you.

Magdalena Suarez Frimkess

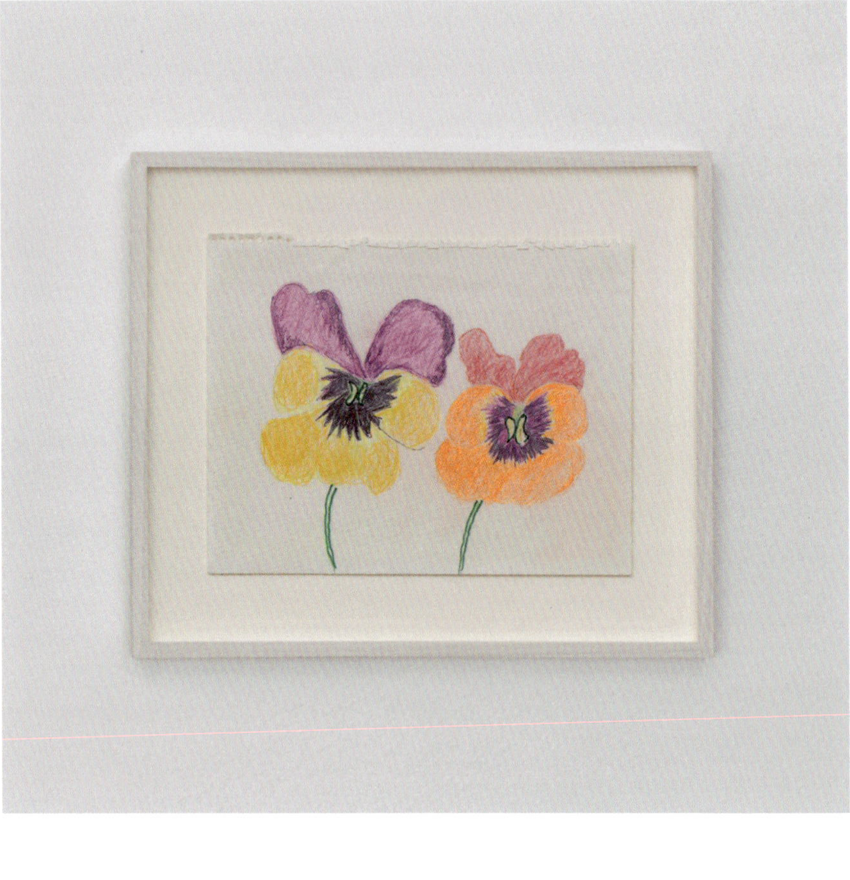

1. *Untitled*, 2002
Glazed ceramic

Courtesy of the artist and kaufmann repetto

2. *Untitled*, 2021
Pen, colored pencil and glitter pen on paper

Courtesy of the artist and private collection and kaufmann repetto

3. *Untitled*, 2021
Glazed ceramic

Courtesy of the artist and kaufmann repetto

The place inside the branches was always opening, not closing

A garden needs for somebody to garden, but
we were braiding birdsong into white noise (boys)
and the green was creeping up on us,
threatening to climb in through an upstairs window.
Standing at an aeolian harp-gate on the hill
the wind plucked a tune that said turn around,
so we did and saw the house was sinking,
swamped by a tidal wave of terrifying green.
Back on land, the wave's underside made caves,
resurrected childhood hiding places in the beech trees
filled with finches' strings of notes to self.
No straight lines, no plants but rampant weeds,
sycamore self-seeding in cracks between footpath and gable
promise to remake this shipwrecked place as forest.

(with lines from David Berman and Jean Valentine)

Swaying, swaying their tops against the sky the trees

I sat out in the garden for the morning,
in danger of lurching into anecdote as metaphor.
Sitting out isn't gardening but isn't writing either.
The poems I had written were failures but dense,
chewy like those rare brownies taken out in time,
though perfection in brownies is failure in poems.
The trees' undersides troubled the shed's tin roof,
which groaned that it's mistaken to fear chainsaws.
That may be true for most tin outhouses,
but the armed and branched among us all
know that just one stumble could be enough
to turn gardening into a scene of massacre,
and dread the sudden density of the air
when the motor buzzes and the sawblade flails.

(with lines from Renee Gladman and Russell Hoban)

Ellen Dillon

Fruits I Have Tasted

I am not waiting for those little yellow cherry plums on the tree I planted eight years ago to ripen before I eat them today. The bare root stick I poked in the ground is now 12' tall and finally producing. I've waited long enough. I go out to find the plumpest yellowest ones, making do with those that have just a shade of green remaining. They're still ok, fine really, but not the sweet sensual drooling down your mouth perfect plum. They will come though. Summer! Last year our coast had a wet cold snap at the moment the plums were blossoming and not a single one fruited anywhere on the coast. When everyone started complaining about it, I didn't feel crazy anymore that I couldn't find any on our trees. Not a single one!

Our big old red cherry plum tree must be at least 24' tall with plum-colored leaves that exactly match the shade of the fruit, rendering them perfectly invisible when they ripen. For the first few years at Salmon Creek Farm I had no idea it produced fruit at all, and then finding them seasons later tried them too early, assuming they weren't for eating. Then the fox started hanging around and climbing the tree in the middle of the day. It was the precise moment of ripeness and she knew. Last year not a single fruit. Four years ago a mysterious bonkers mast year finding the tree so laden with the invisible plum colored orbs that I would be in my nearby cabin and hear large branches snapping and falling under the vast weight. Every day the fruit plumping up, sending branches lower to the ground, and eventually snapping. A bunch of domestically-inclined gays were in residence at the time and we were determined to gather every single fruit and cook them all down as preserves. Our shelves are still lined with them, flavored and labeled, with names like "Cardi Bay" featuring essence of bay leaf.

Today we are about three or four weeks away from our first ripe apples. We have about 50 trees, each a different heritage variety, some beautiful old trees that were planted with the commune in the 70s and others planted by me in 2016. Each sits in a terraced circular bed of its own where we cultivate companion plants, comfrey, perennial herbs, and naturalized wild greens and flowers. Every fall we gather a big group including neighbors and former Salmon Creek Farm communards now in their 70s and 80s for harvests and pressings in late September and early November. The juice sits in glass carboys in my cabin bubbling away for a week during a first violent foamy ferment, with yeasts digesting the sugars and converting it into alcohol, which is what it tastes like after just one week. A vinegar mother is introduced along with some of last year's batch. Then they sit. Just covered cheesecloth to breathe for the first year or so, and then another year or two before it is fully mature. It is our only real product of any quantity, which we don't even sell. I walk into the small room full of carboys in the middle of the winter and imagine the concentrated essence of all of the fruits of last year's orchard that I am inhaling. It's like our currency, trading it with farmer friends for a truckload of compost one year. A gallon is offered to anyone hosting me while traveling. If you added the hours of pruning and tending and feeding and harvesting and pressing and mothering involved throughout the year - all very amateurish, inefficient and non-mechanized - there is no price you could put on it. Just pure gift.

We live two miles from the coast in the redwoods. In the late 1800s this land was logged to the ground. A virgin forest of earth's tallest trees, over 2000 years old, was brought down in a moment. The massive stumps were piled with slash and brush by the loggers and set on fire in hopes of clearing the land for pasture. But when you cut down a redwood it regenerates 2nd growth trees, often in a circle around the original, a faerie ring. Most of those 2nd growth trees were logged again in the 1950s and when the hippies showed up to start their counter culture commune in the 70s it was like a post-industrial landscape of stumps. The trees grow five feet a year and now we have what resembles a forest again, but one that needs care and tending. The virgin redwood forest had around 9-12 massive trees per acre, and those stumps remain as charred monuments across the land. Huckleberries are special companions to the trees, thriving in the understory. Growing out of every ancient stump you will see a mop-head of huckleberry bush sitting on top. In the sun the tiny berries will darken and ripen to delightful flavor. All of the old-timer communards around us strap on the same apparatus to harvest, a yoghurt container with a string around their neck, popping piles of berries in quick gestures right at eye level. My nephews are directed to go outside and pick them when they are bored, I have taught my dog Zucca to forage for them herself, and towards their very peak moment flocks of morning doves will somehow clock it and descend, emptying the bushes of whatever is left.

I have let the raspberries loose to run wild in the most formal front beds of the garden in front of my cabin. At first it was a mistake that I tried to rewind a few years ago, but it was too late, they had laid down their roots and weren't going anywhere. Last fall I cut them back to the ground for seasonal tending, last winter I covered the beds with fresh manure compost, this spring they got a healthy regular watering, and today they have reached a new level of exuberance. Only one or two berries so far but they were perfect. Divine. Deep dark red, perfectly sweet and flavorful. You never know what you're going to get though. A supposedly very desired variety I just planted this season from a reliable source has just started producing the first berries, suggestively plump, enticing deep rich color, plucked at the seemingly perfect moment before they get mushy and disintegrate in your fingers, arriving in your mouth only to discover that they taste like... nothing. Searching for even a hint you realize there is no flavor at all. Also my neighbor's raspberries. Entire beds of them that I greedily run to whenever I visit and they're in season, until the cruel reminder that they are tasteless, what's the use? The fox would never bother.

Salmon Creek Farm is my home since 2014 when I purchased the '70s hippie commune in the coast redwoods of northern California from the last 13 communards. I have since welcomed over 1800 folks through, expanding circles of friends and community. Salmon Creek Arts is starting to offer free programs and will eventually take over operations and ownership.

Graven-stein
Winter Banana
Cox Orange Pippin
Bellflower
Dr. Red Del.
lousy apples
Starkspur Winesap
Golden Delicious
Ornamental plum
Stump
Asian Pear
these may be reversed (?)
Gravenstein
Greening
KING of Tompkins
Pink Pearl
Gravenstein
old vege beds
Tony's Bunk House
Pink Pearl
Russet
Pink Pearl
Roxbury Russet
Pear
plum
cherry
early
mid-season
mid-late
late (Nov)

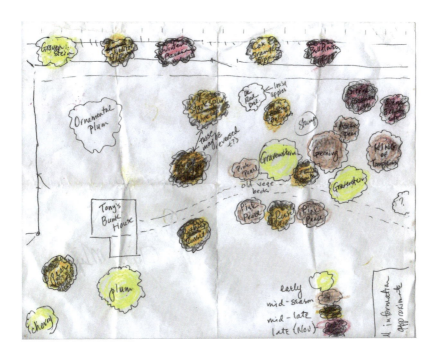

NO SEEDS at beds lining path / future perennials

WILDFLOWERS & COVER CROP at tree circles

W.F.

C.C. at beds

W.F.

WILDFLOWERS

CLOVERS

W.F.

W.F.

W.F.

W.F.

W.F.

CLOVERS

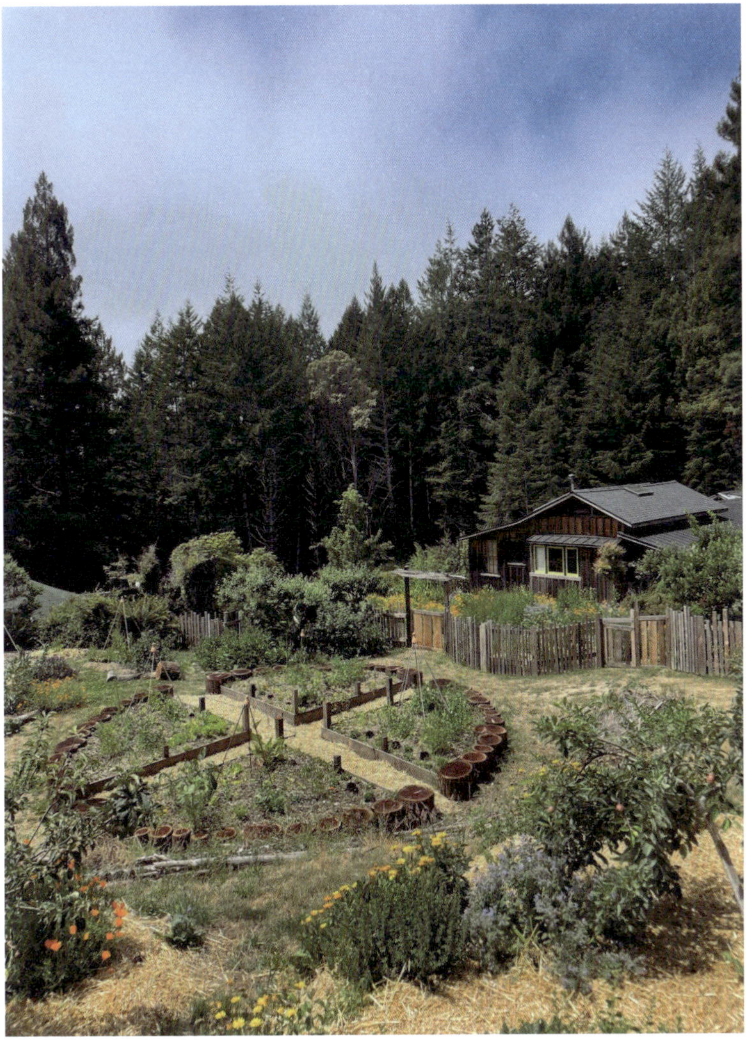

Fritz Haeg

Jamaica Kincaid VENDOR: WINDCLIFF PLANTS   10/19/20
  Professor of Asian and African American Studies
Harvard University
Barker Center, 12 Quincy Street
Cambridge, MA 02138

(617) 496-8543

GENUS species 'Cultivar'	Size	Price	Qty	Total
Agapanthus 'Jamaica Kincaid' (#31)	gal	$35.00	6	$210.00
Paeonia lutea var. ludlowii	gal	$18.00	1	$18.00
Roscoea purpurea HWJK 2020	d4	$18.00	10	$180.00
SUBTOTAL			17	$408.00
SHIPPING VIA USPS PRIORITY MAIL				$162.45
TOTAL DUE				$570.45
PAID BY HERONSWOOD GARDEN				$570.45
TOTAL OWING				$0.00

Jamaica Kincaid

Rosa Mundi

Rosa Mundi - wet, bedraggled, always beautiful.

Of all the plants and flowers and trees in our garden, the one I have the most emotional relationship with is this Rosa Mundi. She tells a story that threads through my life...

My full name is Rosamond, and when I was a baby, my Mum planted a Rosa Mundi to celebrate my arrival. When we moved house, she brought her with us. She survived 4 moves, much-loved, thriving in each new garden. But then things changed...when I was in my late 20s, I became very unwell. I went completely off the rails, sad and lost and confused for quite some time. And for part of that period, I broke contact with my parents. At that very point, with me adrift and my parents marooned in their own distress, Rosa Mundi died. Much later, Mum told me it rocked her to her core, ungrounding her more than anything else had. What if it was a portent? But she didn't give up on me, whatever was going on, and she planted a new Rosa Mundi, desperately willing it to live. Slowly but surely, that's just what happened. And as she grew and flourished in a Northumbrian garden, at the other end of the country, I did just the same. We bloomed. Both of us. Wholeheartedly.

After my parents died, I lifted her from their garden and brought her here. So this Rosa Mundi is that Rosa Mundi, carrying her strength, her fragility and that deep well of endless love and belief and hope. And one of the richest scents of all.

Rosie Hudson

205

206

Jean Perréal
From *Petit Livre d'Amour* by Pierre Sala, c.1500

Transplanting Breadfruit

Poluwat 2500 BC

In the flickering light of the fire, I can see Ku's ribs. He is unsteady on his feet, wavering like a reed. The red paint slashed across his face is too bright against his pale skin. I draw the little ones to my side, to comfort them and myself. They are like two bags of straw. My stomach gnaws.

I have to leave you, he says. *You will all die otherwise.*

He stands there - a god. Who else can he be? This love of mine.

But we will die without you. I hadn't meant to say this aloud.

You will die if I stay.

Something in my chest breaks. The little ones whimper and burrow into my side.

I need your blessing.

I can smell death coming. He has to bury his face into my hair to hear my answer.

Then he raises his hands up toward our twinkling guides. At what point do I realise he is shrinking, no, sinking into the parched earth? His knees, then chest, then shoulders then the mouth I know like the inside of my own, then his eyes white.

The little ones wail and claw at the freshly turned ground where he once stood. I join them lying flat praying to feel him once more. Our tears water his grave. We stay like this for many days and nights, a never ending stream falling from our eyes.

I am sleeping, finally, when I feel a small shake.

Mama.

When I open my blurry eyes, I am unsure what I see. Against the barren, dry, useless earth, is a shoot so green, so alive.

I smile. My lips crack. Ku I say.

South London July 2024

We're sitting side by side on the yellow bench on my concrete balcony. Mum is here for the weekend. Chores are in my mother's blood so I expect this restful Sunday will be anything but.

Green fingers are also in her blood. She spends most of the warmer months in comfy clothes picking, digging, watering, tending her way up and down her large council garden in Leicester.

During winter, without access to her garden, she's sad, de-energised. So I suggest she helps me repot my plants. I need help. Being attentive to non-human species has somehow bypassed my DNA. I can just about keep my self-sufficient succulents alive. Truth be known, I'm a little scared of plants. They know things I don't. They react. They grow in unsuspecting ways or suddenly keel over, wilt, crisp up. Now their roots are straining out of their plant pot homes. I'm better with things that can communicate their needs in words. I don't want to hurt them and I might. I watch as she expertly gathers old newspaper, bags of compost, watering can, gravel. She's 84 and I'm 54 but I still feel the same level of reassurance I felt as a child as she calmly sought out the spiders in dark corners and took them tenderly outside. She is much more at peace with that which lies beyond our human world than I.

Portsmouth 1789

An improbable hero arrives on a ship called Bounty - a head gardener from Kew Gardens. Excitedly, he unwraps his leather case to show the crew beautiful illustrations of the Breadfruit. You see, they'll soon be casting off from Portsmouth to travel halfway across the world to an isolated island in the middle of the Pacific. There they will pick some saplings before journeying another 5000 miles to deposit them in Jamaica. This audacious voyage is by order of King George who requires a high yielding food plant to feed his slaves.

The ill-fated journey makes history thanks to the tyrannous Captain Bligh who treats his crew like plantation chattel - whipping them if he senses any attempt to scupper the safe transportation of the precious plants. Mutiny on the Bounty, the dramatisation of this fateful trip, makes for a startling film. Produced in 1962, it offers a rare insight into the cruelty of the colonial psyche. Not only that but taking centre place alongside big screen names like Marlon Brando and Trevor Howard is the humble Breadfruit. In one memorable scene, mutinous crew members begin dumping the cargo overboard, littering the azure Pacific Ocean with seemingly hundreds of elegant green shrubs.

Ultimately Bligh doesn't let a bunch of pesky mutineers get in the way of his life's legacy. A few years later he successfully completes the trip. However before reaching Jamaica, he stops off at St Vincent, a small volcanic island in the Caribbean and drops off a plant or two. The Breadfruit goes on to become St Vincent's national dish and St Vincent goes on to become my family home after my ancestors are transported from Africa on another kind of ship.

Breadfruit in ancient Polynesian lore represents knowledge. So unbeknownst to that in-fighting crew, they were in fact transferring knowledge to this tiny island just as the captains of the slave ships were transporting other kinds of knowledge in the bodies and stories of the people they carry.

South London July 2024

I ask my mother where her love of gardening comes from. She tells me that it began as a child 'Back Home' in St Vincent. Her grandmother gave her the task of watering the garden. It was a job she liked. This chore was more preferable to other onerous jobs like selling bread before school which involved walking miles with a basket on her head. Like many Caribbean girls in the 1950s, Mum was put to work early in life. It was as if the primary reason to parent girls was to breed an obliging workforce. But as descendants of the enslaved, women were often sole breadwinners, home makers and child rearers, so help was probably necessary.

The plants from 'Back Home' that mum speaks of most are the ones that provided sustenance - Mangoes, Bananas, Dasheen, Eddoes and Breadfruit. She talks of land rather than gardens - plots they cultivated and harvested once a year. Leftover produce would be shared with neighbours. When the harvest season was over and the food ran out, they would go hungry once again.

Austronesia 2500 BC

Long before the Bounty's tumultuous trip to the Polynesian islands, the Breadfruit was already well travelled. Around 2500 BC, during the Austronesian expansion, people sailed canoes from New Guinea, Maluku Islands and the Philippines to Oceania taking Breadfruit plants with them.

One of the Micronesian islands called Poluwat had a sacred lore organised into five categories: war, magic, meetings, navigation, and breadfruit. The story of how the breadfruit came to be centres on the god of War, Ku who, pretending to be mortal, marries and has a family. During a dreadful famine, he magically turns himself into a Breadfruit tree to save his family from starvation. Thanks to Ku and the people who crossed seas and centuries to transplant, domesticate and hybridise this plant, Breadfruit now feeds half the world.

St Vincent 1765

Founded in 1765, St Vincent has the oldest botanical gardens in the western hemisphere. The arrival of Captain Bligh's famous Breadfruit helped, as did the rich volcanic soil and the broader colonial project to turn seized Caribbean islands into growing laboratories. As plantations worked by enslaved Africans grew across the islands, so did botanical gardens. Here Island Surgeon Botanists would test out indigenous and imported food, commercial and medicinal plants to benefit Britain. St. Vincent's Botanical Garden was especially designed to cultivate new plant species from the East.

Then, as now, plants are respected as migratory vessels of knowledge. It was understood that by uprooting, transplanting, cross-pollinating and germinating that knowledge, more life could be enhanced. Humans are migratory vessels of knowledge too. Small amounts of money were offered by the British for some of that indigenous knowledge to aid those early experiments.

If my grandmother had been around then, she may have made a pretty penny. She is the one who held the healing plant knowledge in my family. She knew which plants to boil to make the Bush teas to cure certain ailments. As a pre-teen, I remember one mortifying afternoon, Granny stalked around our garden in Leicester gathering dandelions to make me a bath to cure my period pains. Dandelions were a disgusting weed that, if twirled between your legs, would make you pee, and worse than that, all our neighbours could see and hear her! I smile now thinking how we faced off in the garden, separated by 4000 miles of cultural difference. Now Granny has gone and I am left only too aware how rootless I am without her knowledge.

July 2024 South London

I don't often hear Mum speak of St Vincent's flowering plants, so I ask if she had any favourites. She pauses. She doesn't remember the names. There was a yellow one they colloquially called Buttercups. Buttercups is, most likely, not the official name and most certainly does not refer to the delicate English weed that, as a child, we used to twizzle under our chins to see if we liked butter or not.

Mum seems to be getting a little impatient with my questions. It's not always easy raising the subject of the past with Caribbean people. Too much blood has seeped into that beautiful land, too much trauma sewn into the skin of the people. Survival meant avoiding looking directly at the horror and legacy of plantation slavery. Once upon a time looking and naming could result in vicious punishments like having salt and maggots rubbed into raw, lashed wounds. Burying the past is an art that has been mastered by many from that region.

And yet I am called to dig up the past, to excavate the genus of the seed that lies inside of me. I go seeking in old 1960s films and lengthy hours tracing internet pixels back across the seas.

So instead I tell her about how St Vincent's botanical gardens is the oldest in the western hemisphere and that the epic tale of Mutiny on the Bounty starred the humble Breadfruit.

She's delighted by these stories and I wonder if, in fact, my mum does share my interest in the past but, when young, lacked the internet to quietly consult.

In return she shows me how to turn a plant pot sideways and hold the plant gently by its stem. She taps the bottom of the pot until the soil begins to shift and the plant begins to slide out. She gently loosens the earth around the roots, tenderly brushing away the dirt until the roots stand bare. She decisively pulls away the old depleted bark-like roots until the tendrils of new ones emerge. She shows me just the amount of gravel to add to the bottom of the pot, and generously tops up with fresh, rich, dark compost. She carves out a hole and beds the old plant in new soil, pressing down softly.

2190 Artocarpus Altilis, Sunflower Galaxy

The young woman waves her hand over the console and the Wardian box glides out of its encasement. I can tell by the condensation on the inside of the glass that, thankfully, the humidity maintained throughout the flight from Earth.

She's beautiful, my young companion says.

The young Breadfruit plant stands healthy at almost a metre high. The stem looks strong and a few thick serrated leaves are deep green with no hint of browning. We look at each other and smile.

Do you know how the Breadfruit came to be? I ask her.

She was born here on Altilis. I can tell by the soft blueish tint to her taut skin and her slightly enlarged eyes. My own skin carries the tell-tale wrinkles indicating that my home is 20 million light years away. Her eyes widen. She likes to hear the stories from Back Home.

No I don't but I'd love to.

Well, I begin. *There was once a god called Ku …*

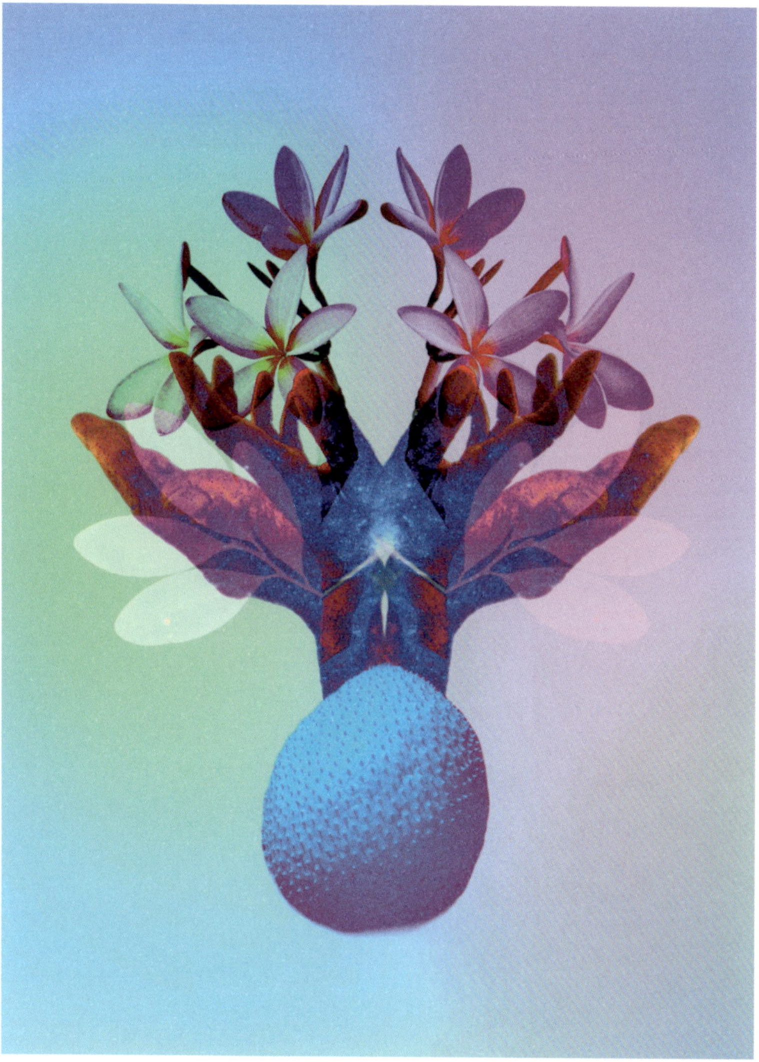

Gaylene Gould

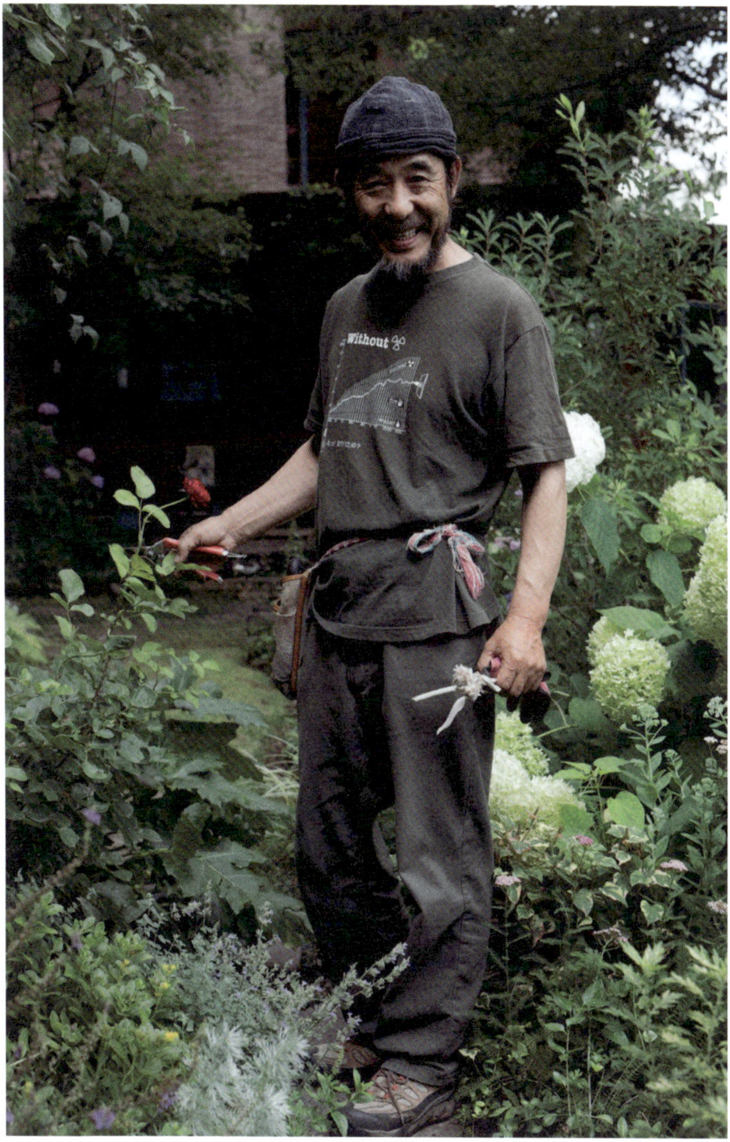
Without

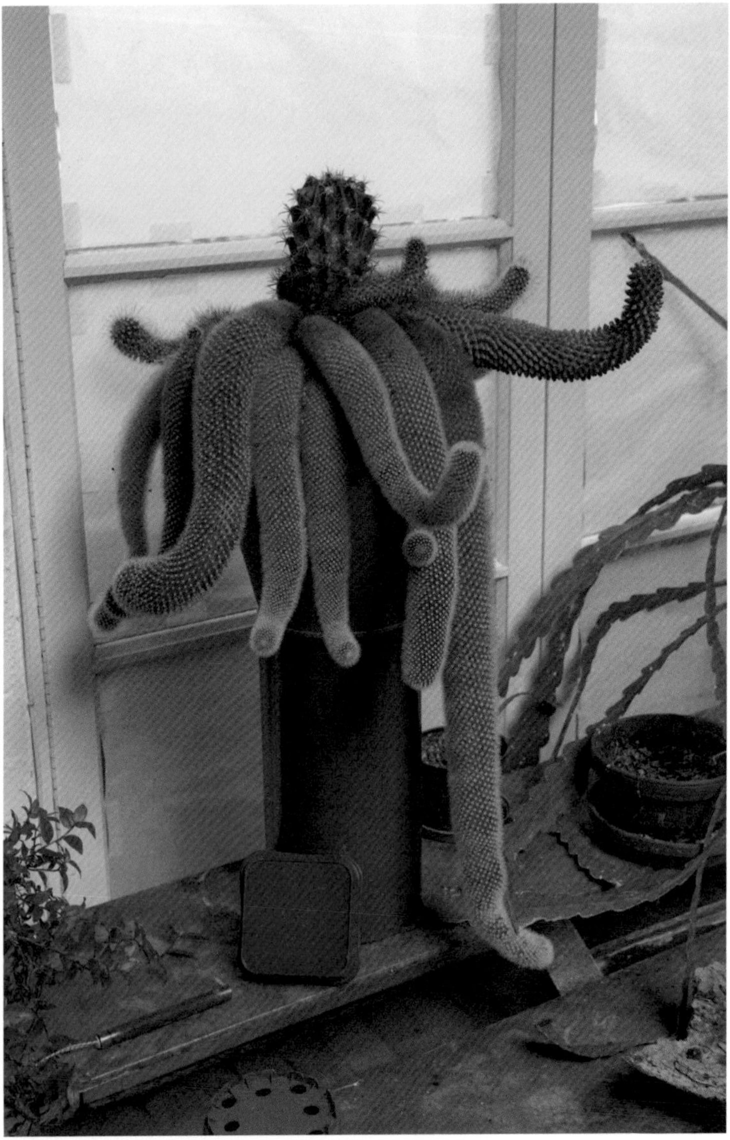

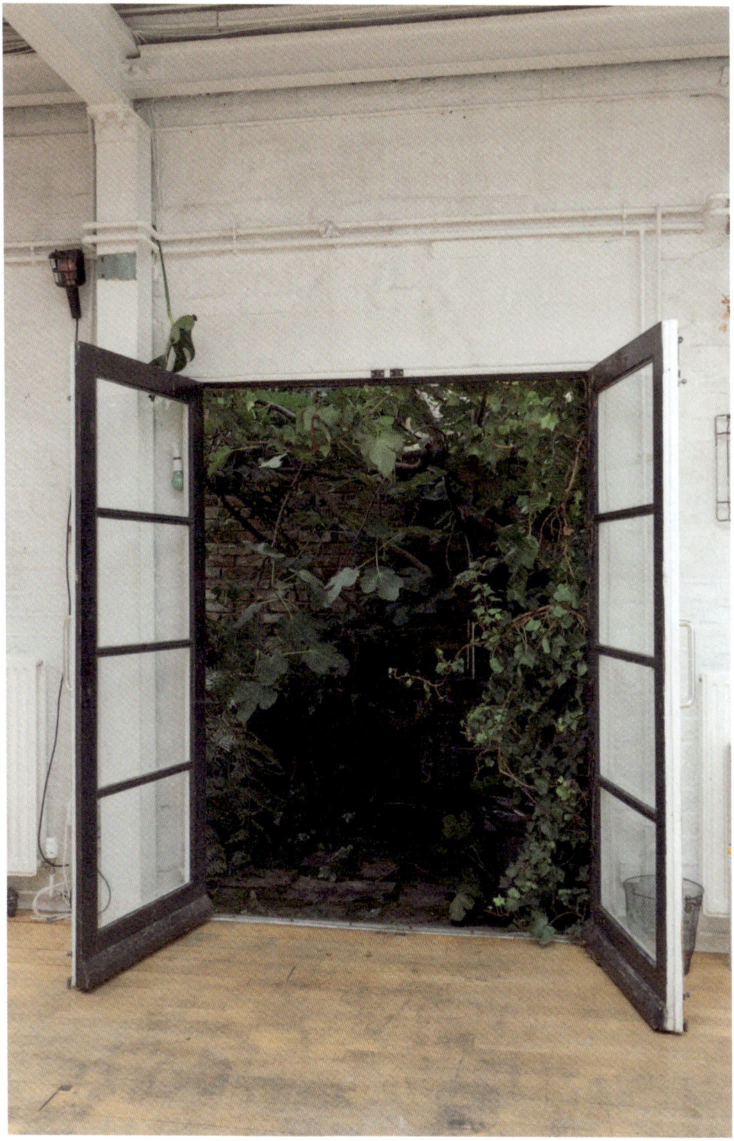

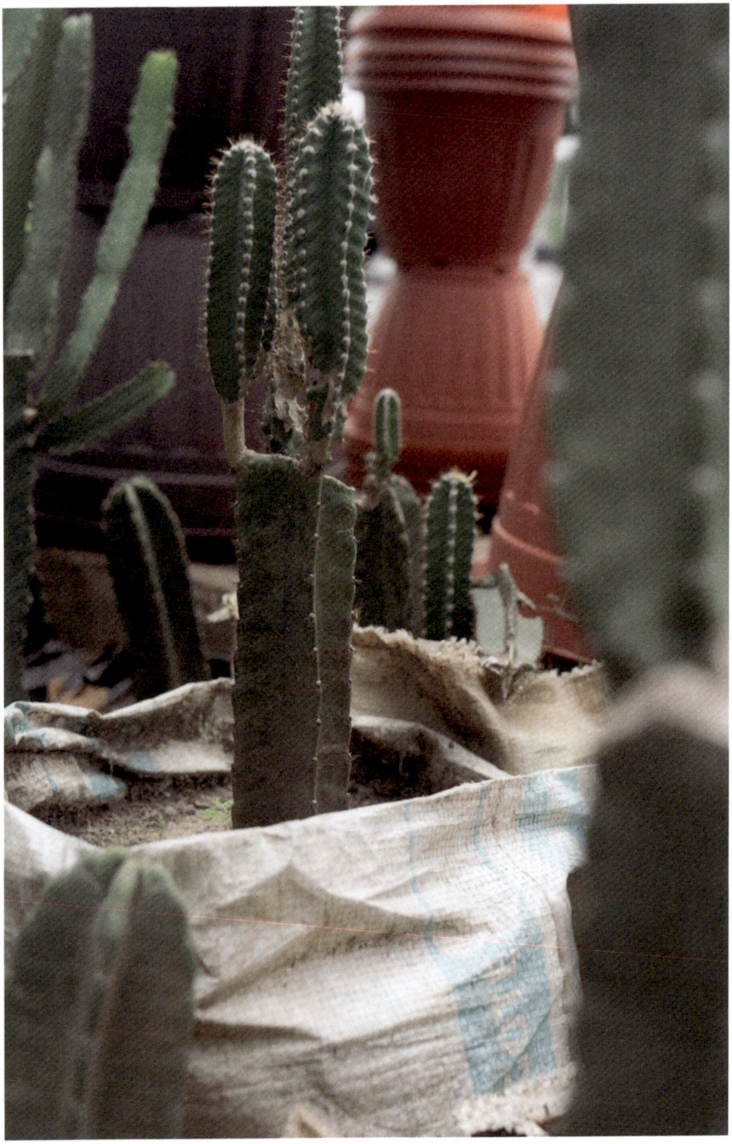

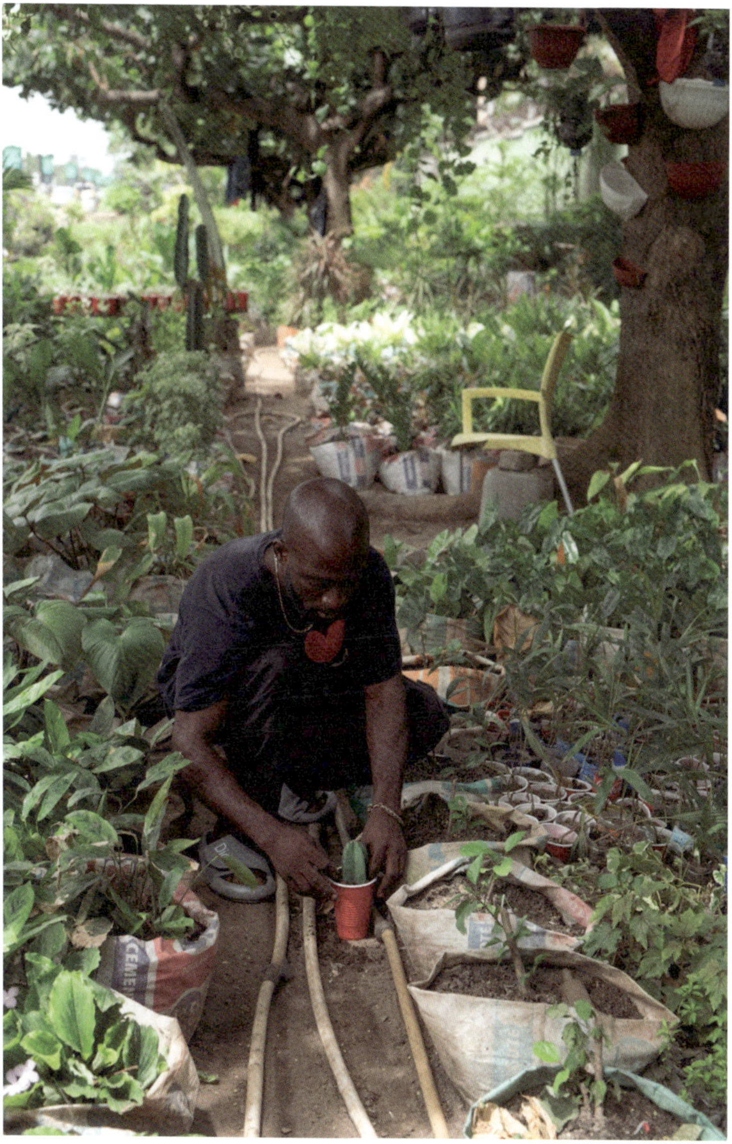

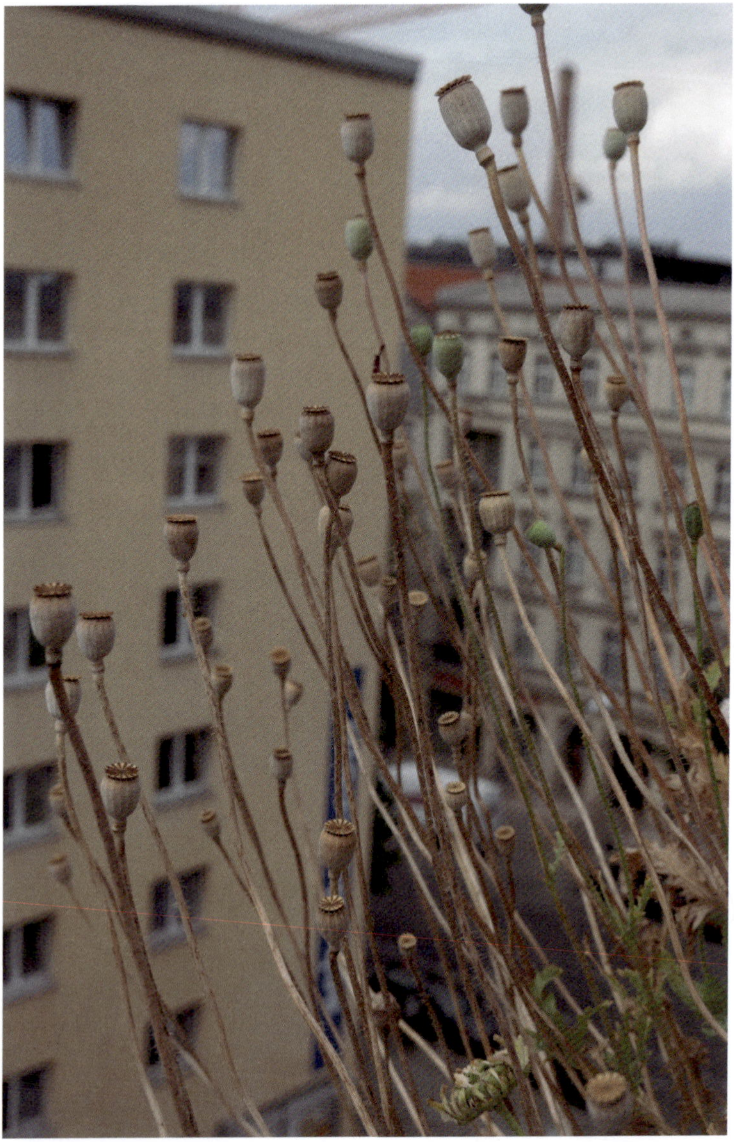

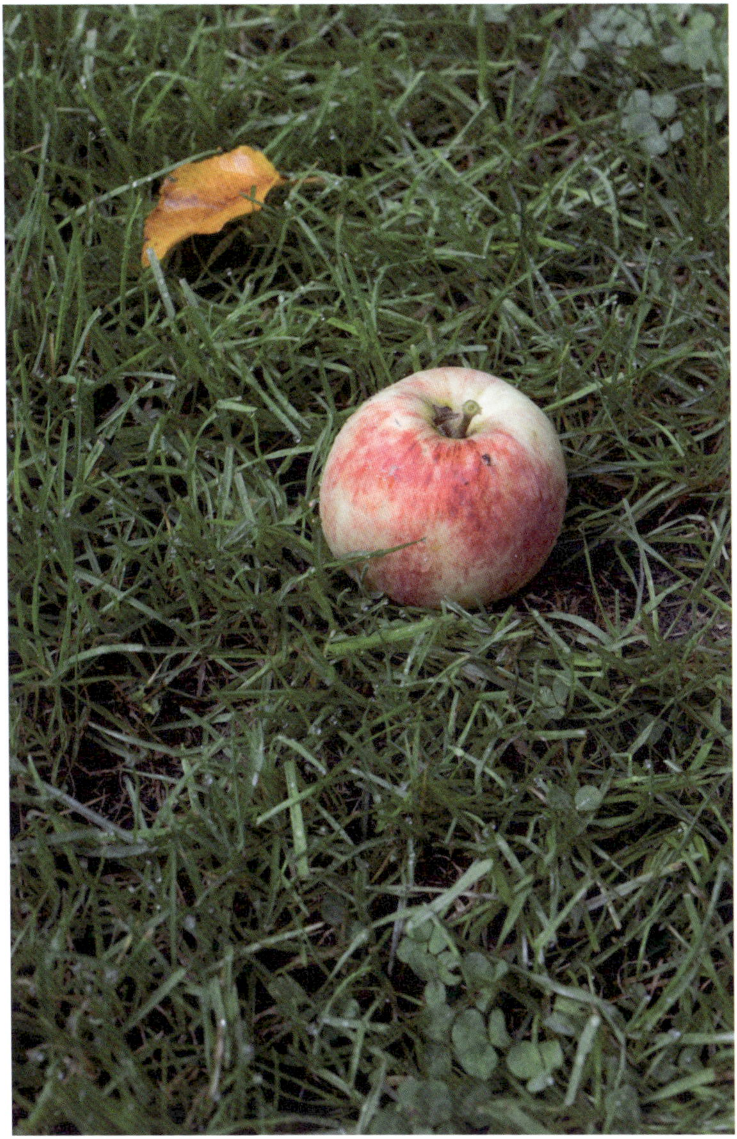

Wolfgang Tillmans

Plants flowers in the garden

It was a Social Education lesson, the kind you could tell even the teacher couldn't be arsed with. The object of the exercise was to arrange an imaginary pupil's list of extracurricular activities into a timetable, to teach us time management ahead of exams that actually mattered.

Plants flowers in the garden, read Mr Muir from the textbook. It's Kieran McKechnie, someone called out immediately. Everyone laughed, Mr Muir laughed. I probably laughed too.

I was thirteen that spring, the year of my obsession with the solar-powered water feature. It came from one of the catalogues that proliferated in the weekend papers; microwave egg poachers, discreet incontinence pants. A plastic circle in a blue glazed bowl, it bravely spurted six inches into the air when the Glasgow sun shone directly on it, stopping the moment a cloud passed over. I'd elevated it on a plinth of precariously stacked yellow bricks left over from the extension, planting an ivy at its base to hide their brashness in time.

The fountain was the focal point of the narrow strip of garden alongside our end-of-terrace, shielded from the main road by a thinning privet hedge. I'd contrived this vista around a picture in one of my grandmother's old gardening books. In a stone-walled garden, climbing roses tumbled over arches and Alchemilla mollis seeded itself between York stone, framing a heavily lichened sundial of some antiquity. I used artistic licence for my version, paving it myself in precast Cotswold Buff from B&Q, laid wonkily on sand. Balance and dignity were brought by a pair of marguerites flanking the path in bright new terracotta pots; they'd soon age with a bit of milk splashed on, though the sticky rectangles left by the £6.99 stickers remained to compromise their patina. The lady's mantle was just the same.

I'd beg my mum to drive out to the retail park ('Where are your friends?'), try convincing her we needed pre-formed topiary or a tree fern, knew it was futile. I policed the colour schemes of bedding plants; the thrill of a White Garden six pack of pelargonium, petunia and lobelia, just like Sissinghurst. I wanted to plant a rose to scramble up the gable end, 'Albéric Barbier' or 'Mme. Alfred Carrière', but a cracked grey concrete path hugged the wall and I was banned from drilling the pointing. Instead a selection of out-of-scale shrubs were squashed into a 3 foot wide border – an assertive golden elder, sharp against the blue bowl, a sad spiraea kept only for its maturity – to section off this inferior path from my flagged one, separating my space entirely. I was obsessed with the idea of enclosure, a hortus conclusus in which I would remove myself from the world. I'd take a chair and the Sunday supplements, nicked from under my dad's nose before he disappeared with them into the bathroom, to my confined corridor, as close to the fountain as I could get without overshadowing its solar panel, smugly acknowledging the relaxing tinkle even as it barely registered over the traffic.

Christopher Lloyd in the Guardian magazine on a Saturday; the thrill of dahlias and cannas clashing in his ripped-up-rose garden, the hints of worlds I'd yet to fathom, far removed from the Calvinism of BBC Scotland's Beechgrove Garden. House and garden saturated the media then and I lapped it up, the era of chucking out your chintz, Home Front, Ground Force, and Changing Rooms; names weirdly redolent of stiff upper lips and cold showers. A garden shed makeover competition for kids. I remember the winning design so clearly, a 6x4 shiplap transformed into a bijou post-Bloomsbury Versailles, all cobalt and burnt orange paint with gilded stick-on mouldings, the rococo panelling framing bright yellow plastic sunflowers. Its creator was a boy my age. I can still feel how I recoiled from the recognition.

Sunflowers
orange gerberas
wavy lime green vases
the Spice Girls
Push Pops
the underwear in the Next Directory.

Real sanctuary was the school holidays. We spent them in Nairn. Grannie's garden was vast compared with ours, a real walled garden, albeit behind a 1930s bungalow and bounded by breezeblocks. But at the end was the lovely pink sandstone wall of the big house beyond, a relic from the town's Brighton of the North heyday. This was the backdrop to a proper herbaceous border of campanulas, delphiniums and great flourishing lavenders. In the far corner was the veg patch, given over to potatoes, peas, gooseberries and a glorious row of raspberry canes, still my favourite fruit but never quite so good as straight from the bush on a quiet July afternoon by yourself.

The veg abutted the hidey hole, a secret place parents were banned from, where Grannie and I sat just the two of us at a picnic table, eating tablet and shelling peas. Her funny turns of phrase: my wee loon, gey queer. She taught me to say Primula denticulata. Grannie's boy. There's a photo of me at three, with an auburn fringe and a Stork margarine tub of Michaelmas daisies and Sweet Williams on my lap, our entry to a competition in the Seamen's Hall. With Grannie I sowed my first nasturtiums, still going strong when I returned in October for the tattie holidays, a miracle.

Years later, the two of us in her kitchen and Emmerdale's on.

He's one of them.
One of what? I knew though.

You know,
abnormal.

You heard about Brighton
Manchester
Section 28
The Admiral Duncan
Queer as Folk
on the 70s fake wood-veneered TV set of a dead great aunt in the shared bedroom, index finger poised over the off button.

Plants flowers in the garden.

Spring, the present, the east of England. Rainbows in sash windows. The garden I'm working in, a big institution, is closed, down to critical care only. I'm at a loose end. I zoom my friends, draw up timetables I never stick to, finally finish *Modern Nature*. I'm losing sleep. I give up on HIIT workouts with Instagram personal trainers and think about messaging an ex.

The order arrives at last. Even now you hope for the best when sowing seeds, never quite believe it'll work. First through are the zinnias, tentatively pushing up, coat still attached. Soon enough green pinpricks pepper most of the trays; promises of bronze fennel, purple kale, Salvia patens, Rhodochiton atrosanguineas and, in palest lemon now, sunflowers.

I'm making a garden for me again, in a narrow border outside the tied cottage door. I make obelisks from pea sticks, place pebbles like Derek while I wait for my charges to grow. Plant a dahlia called 'Tartan'; flirt with kitsch but try to dodge irony. Still evenings alone in the polytunnel with chaffinches and the scent of lilac, pricking out, potting on, seeing the whole thing through. It hasn't felt like this in years.

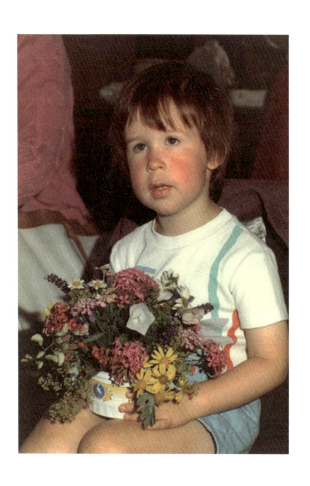

Colin Stewart

Derek Jarman
Landscape with a Blue Pool, 1967
Oil on canvas

© Estate of Derek Jarman
Courtesy of Arts Council Collection, Southbank Centre

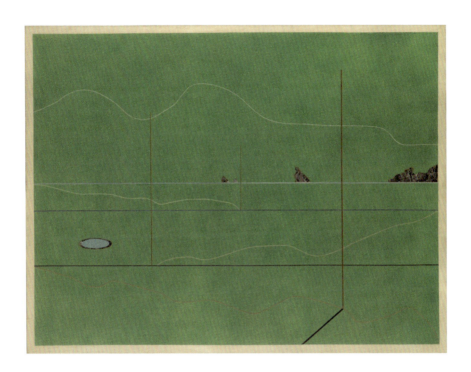

237

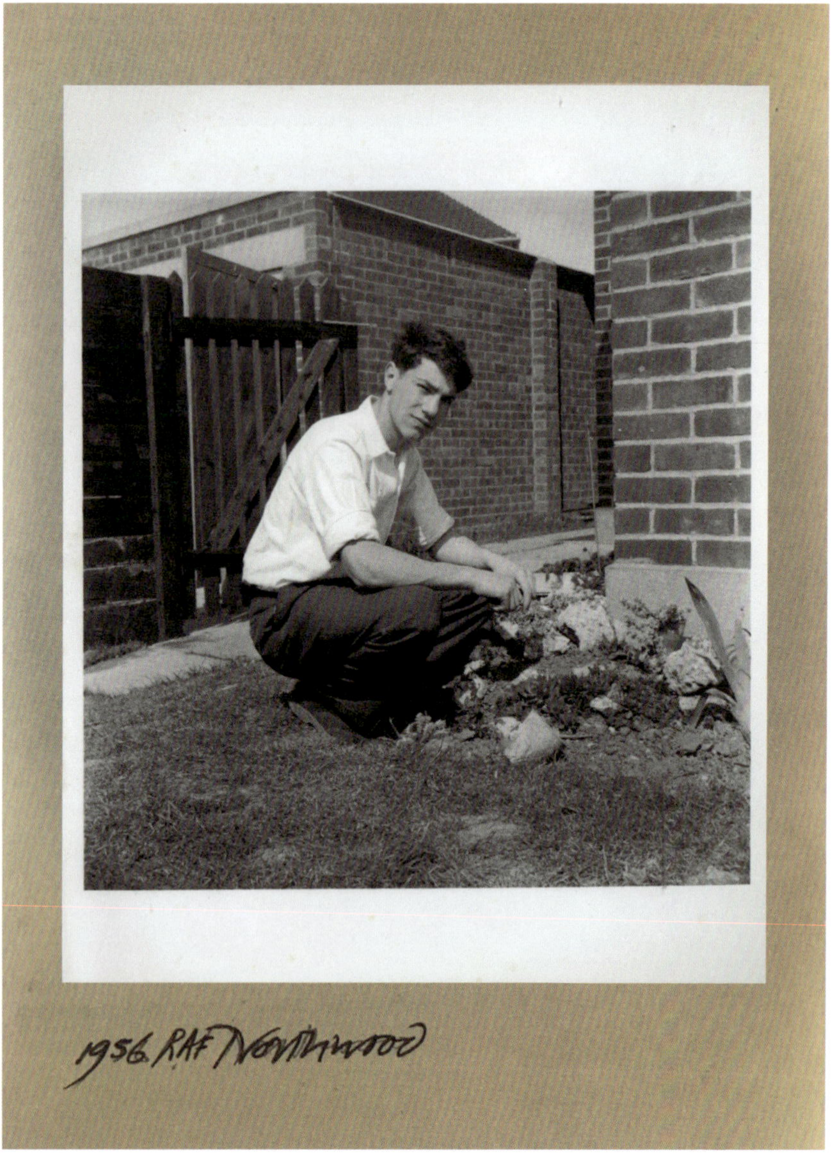
1956. RAF Northwood

Derek Jarman gardening at RAF Northwood, 1956

Courtesy of the Keith Collins Will Trust

Siobhan Liddell
A page from *A Hundred Million Years of Nectar Dances*
by Richard Jarette, Green Writers Press, 2015

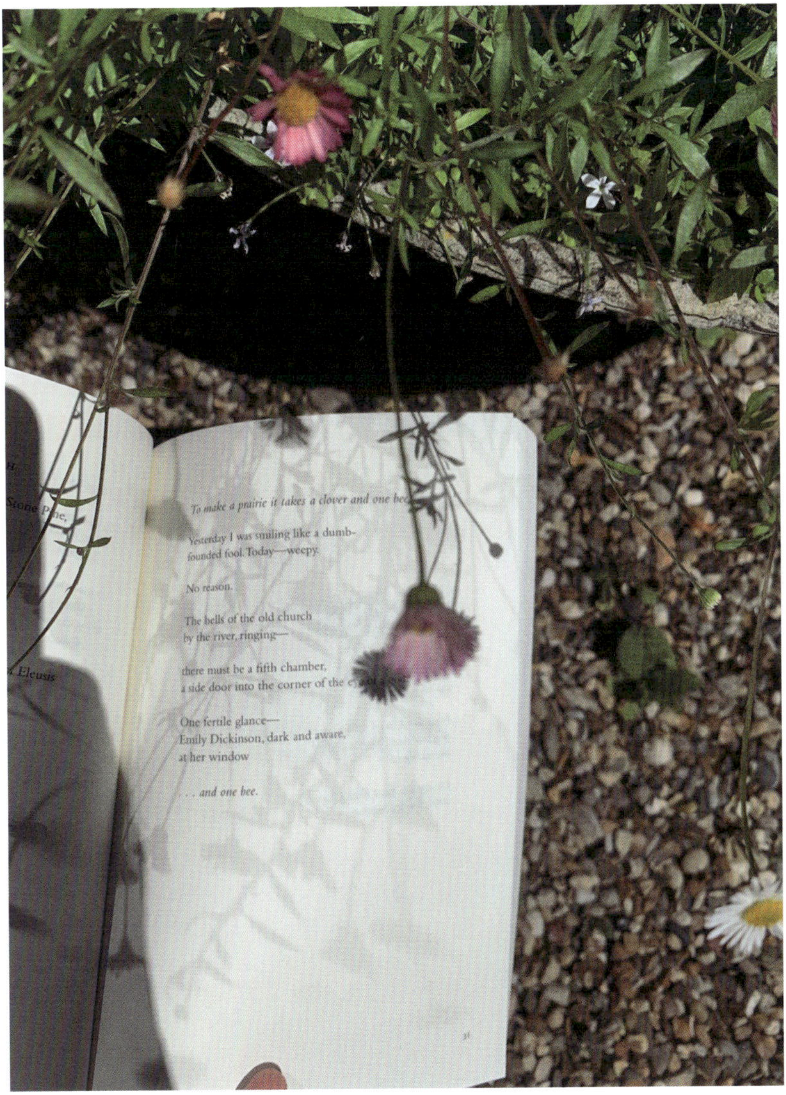
To make a prairie it takes a clover and one bee
Yesterday I was smiling like a dumb-
founded fool. Today—weepy.
No reason.
The bells of the old church
by the river, ringing—
there must be a fifth chamber,
a side door into the corner of the e
One fertile glance—
Emily Dickinson, dark and aware,
at her window
. . . and one bee.
Stone Pine,
Eleusis

84. I Remember a Clear Morning

I remember a clear morning in the Ninth Month when it had been raining all night. Despite the bright sun, dew was still dripping from the chrysanthemums in the garden. On the bamboo fences and criss-cross hedges I saw tatters of spider webs; and where the threads were broken the raindrops hung on them like strings of white pearls. I was greatly moved and delighted.

As it became sunnier, the dew gradually vanished from the clover and the other plants where it had lain so heavily; the branches began to stir, then suddenly sprang up of their own accord. Later I described to people how beautiful it all was. What most impressed me was that they were not at all impressed.

Sei Shōnagon
From *The Pillow Book*, c. 1002

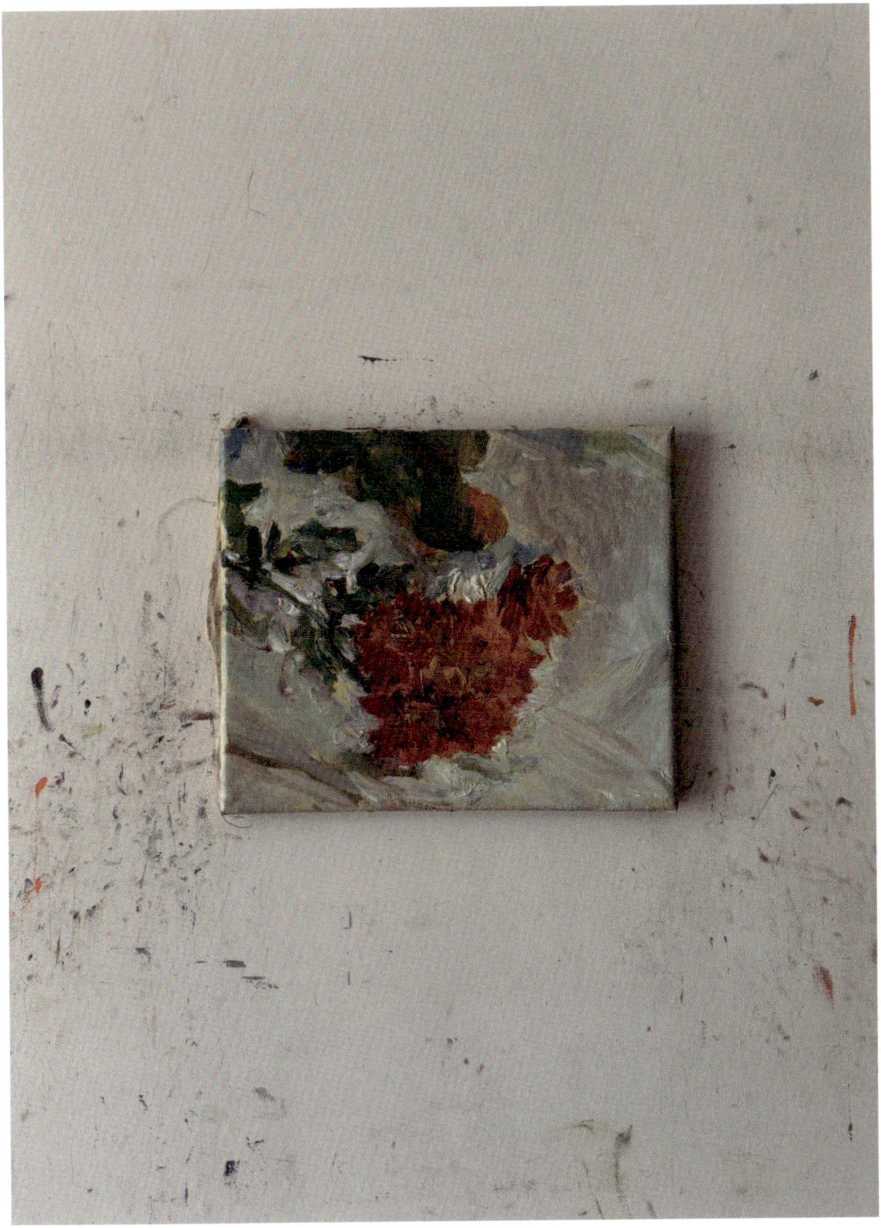

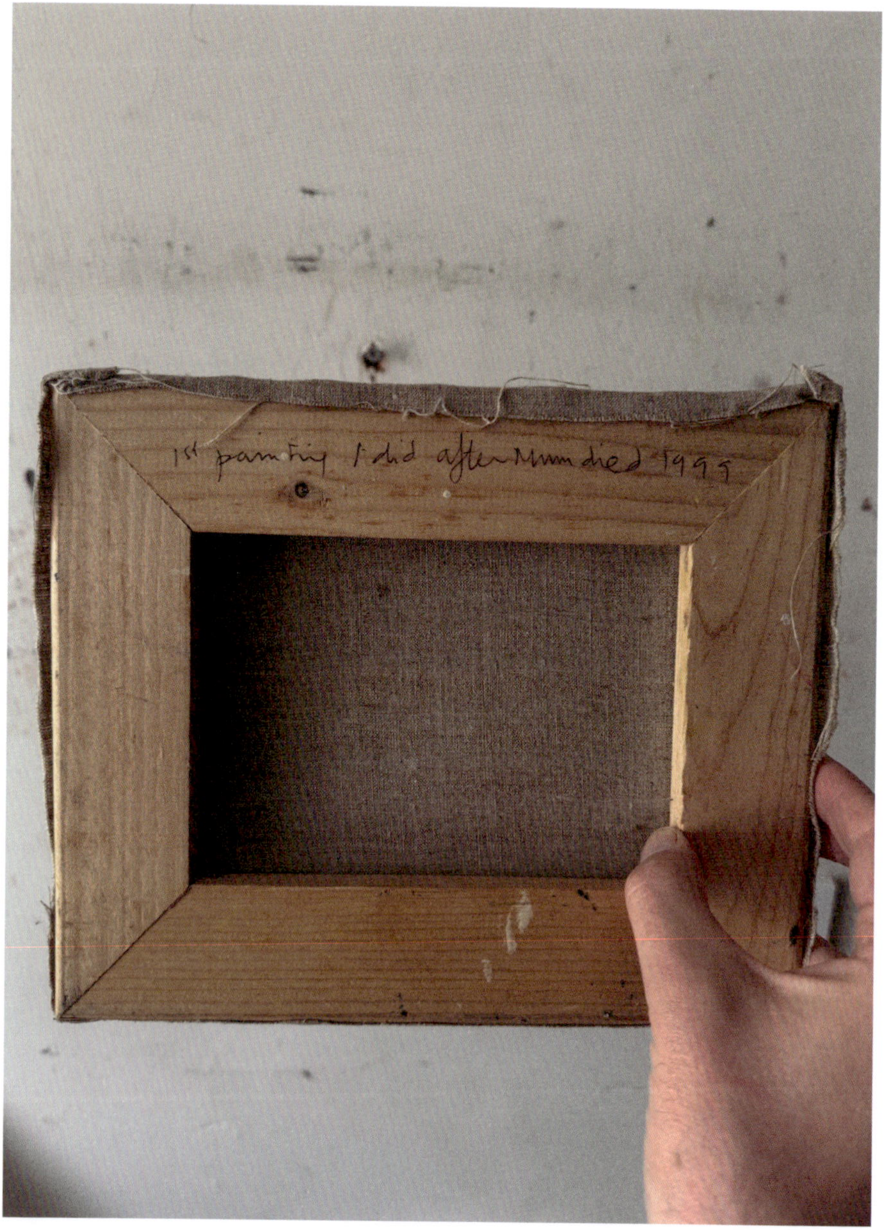
1st painting I did after Mum died 1999

Pat Porter
1st painting I did after Mum died, **1999**
Oil on canvas
Photographed by Charlie Porter

Arnold Circus is a community garden built on the rubble of the Jago. At the end of the 19th century, a whole district of slums in Shoreditch, east London, was demolished to create the Boundary Estate, one of the earliest examples of government-funded public housing. At the centre, the leftover rubble became the foundations for a raised garden crowned by a bandstand. The soil is terrible.

By the late 20th century, the gardens had fallen into decline. It became known as a place of homophobic violence. At the beginning of the 21st century, punters at the nearby gay bar The George and Dragon would tell each other: don't cut through Arnold Circus. A group of local residents took action and formed The Friends of Arnold Circus. They began the regeneration of the gardens. The mood soon lifted. Today, the gardens are glorious.

There are over twenty London Plane trees on the gardens. The volunteers of Arnold Circus mulch their leaves in four leaf bins, along with all other green matter from the gardens. Plane leaves are often seen as unwieldy plates, but, with some turning and watering through the year, they break down. In this photograph are the hands of volunteers Andy Willoughby and Loucas Louca on 12 July 2024, turning one of the leaf bins. By the time you read this, the resulting mulch will be nourishing the beds.

Charlie Porter

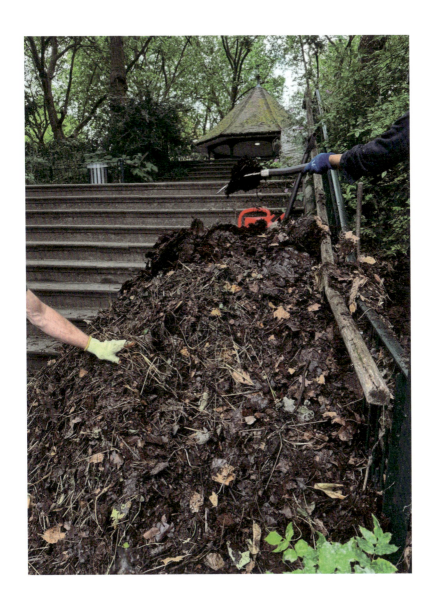

On the Hill of Tara

On the Hill of Tara, nobody owns the green
Nobody hesitates to sit on the grass
Under a clear sky that barely lasts
And what about our jeans
Mom, we are in the Land of Troubles not the Land of the Occupied
Grass stains are the stains of the free
At least, we can do this here

On the Hill of Tara, nobody owns the green
The green surrounds us, but never chases us like those back home
Some say the Troubles have ended
Others say the Troubles are still here
It is mid June and we are all awaiting the sun in despair
Until Tara shows us the warm Daffodil

Back home, we only see one type of green
Shades of green are reserved to those living behind that wall
A wall they do not even see as they swim in *our* sea
And that sea they see, we never get to see
Except in a dream
Their green is so serene
Our green is that type of green: heavy, dark, rotten, nauseous, dead bodies,
stained in blood, our blood, inhumane

Back home, we only see one type of green
They tell us that no green exists beyond their military regime
That no green exists beyond their greenish muddy boots as they invade our
homes and dreams
That no green exists beyond their F-16
That no green exists beyond the uprooted olive trees
We hear them in disdain
So, we search and see

And then we find that
And then we find that
Even under occupation, the flowers bloom as they face the ugly wall
Even under occupation, the sun continues to rise as more of us die
Even under occupation, mothers insist on bearing more children
Only for them to mourn their babies under a black sky
We are a people who try to see beyond that type of green
But oftentimes, the green is too much green

On the Hill of Tara, your children look exactly like our children
Our children too come in blue and green eyes
Our children too can skip around as they stick out their tongue in the rain
But instead, they bite their tongue as the bombs fall on them
Our children too love their cinnamon rolls
But instead, they sell them to feed their families during famine and war

Back home, we only see one type of green
And they will tell our children too that no green exists beyond their regime
But our children shall not fall for this
For who will grow the next olive tree
Who will preserve the *Zaytoon/Olives* and *Tin/Figs*

One summer at the checkpoint, I saw a different type of green:
Half-open olive eyes that could not see clearly what we could see
The sun knows its people
Those who stand facing her no matter how severe
Those who greet her with open arm and happy tears
Those whose skin never breaks apart as it kisses them here and there
And that is how I know, that our children will live to see all sorts of green
as they swim in our sea

On the Hill of Tara, nobody owns the green
Nobody hesitates to sit on the grass
Under a clear sky that barely lasts
And what about our jeans
Mom, we are in the Land of Troubles not the Land of the Occupied
Grass stains are the stains of the free
At least, we can do this here

Baha Ebdeir

What is this little guy's job in the world. If this little guy dies does the world know? Does the world feel this? Does something get displaced? If this little guy dies does the world get a little lighter? Does the planet rotate a little faster? If this little guy dies, without his body to shift the currents of air, does the air flow perceptibly faster? What shifts if this little guy dies? Do people speak language a little bit differently? If this little guy dies does some little kid somewhere wake up with a bad dream? Does an almost imperceptible link in the chain snap? Will civilization stumble?

David Wojnarowicz
What is this little guy's job in the world, 1990
Silver gelatin print

What is this little guy's job in the world. If this little guy dies does the world know? Does the world feel this? Does something get displaced? If this little guy dies does the world get a little lighter? Does the planet rotate a little faster? If this little guy dies, without his body to shift the currents of air, does the air flow perceptibly faster? What shifts if this little guy dies? Do people speak language a little bit differently? If this little guy dies does some little kid somewhere wake up with a bad dream? Does an almost imperceptible link in the chain snap? Will civilization stumble?

255

In First Tuft

So be it bell bee lift medick black reliquary
fumitory cloven zigzag agree proud bee scout
provoked teasel, we'd hawk orange sleeping
licit brighten maybe buck past night eye win
shadoof arrested honour honied gathered thorn
apsidal mantle; bee better supple wax oddment
reside around torment until tillage phrasing
candour in first tuft. Will to be absconded,
bit over frugal step foot bird gibbous seek
to wade speed sweet braid brigantine western
grass-wrack oh willow lighten one obol fescue
half scruple rueful strife lost foil sunken
flag yellow alchemic, well to speed, spelling
alex and erstwhile milder dewfall flow gentle
vernal enjoy unravel, glove wolf to foxy off
must to travel figment worth welsh popularise
astonish crop to stretch. Stitch, worshipful
dropwort walking basset mallow elbow winding
ill-met crane billet chalk hill, fugal would
sorrel sorrowful meadow scented entreat sweet
fasten shaded if rift, listed thrift on hold
bed strewn mown tufted edgeways led by nature
hardly felt, the kind you are, square spear
new-mint tway robert herb blood fortune meet
fate hay rattle settle; white bryony bees
terse creeping wrack grapple miller dusty.

J. H. Prynne
From *Passing Grass Parnassus*, Face Press, 2020

Contributors
in order of appearance

Saadi
Joe Brainard
John Wieners
Chantal Joffe
Sui Searle
Lee Mary Manning
Edward Thomasson
Philip Hoare
Ana Mendieta
William Blake
Jo McKerr
Tabboo!
Elisabeth Kley
Palestinian Heirloom
  Seed Library
Ian Patterson
Jamie Reid
Gerry Dalton
Kuba Ryniewicz
Jeremy Lee
Lubaina Himid
Olivia Laing
Matt Wolf
Unknown artist
Scott Treleaven
Claire Ratinon
Dan Pearson
Huw Morgan
Jonny Bruce
Green Guerillas

Laura Joy
Eileen Myles
Rosemary Mayer
Bernadette Mayer
Unknown artist
Hussein Omar
Joy Gregory
John Clare
Alison Lloyd
Hilary Lloyd
Lisa Robertson
Alys Fowler
Sarah Wood
Magdalena Suarez Frimkess
Ellen Dillon
Fritz Haeg
Jamaica Kincaid
Rosie Hudson
Jean Perréal
Gaylene Gould
Wolfgang Tillmans
Colin Stewart
Derek Jarman
Siobhan Liddell
Sei Shōnagon
Pat Porter
Charlie Porter
Baha Ebdeir
David Wojnarowicz
J. H. Prynne

A Garden Manifesto

Olivia Laing and Richard Porter (eds.)

Cover artwork: David Wojnarowicz, *What is this little guy's job in the world,* 1990, silver gelatin print © *Estate of David Wojnarowicz* Courtesy of the Estate of David Wojnarowicz and P.P.O.W, New York

Published in the U.K. by Pilot Press, 2024

978-1-0687586-0-7

www.pilotpress.co.uk/catalogue